JAN
MORRIS

FROM THE FOUR
CORNERS

PENGUIN BOOKS

PENGUIN BOOKS

Published by the Penguin Group. Penguin Books Ltd, 27 Wrights Lane, London
w8 5tz, England. Penguin Books USA Inc., 375 Hudson Street, New York, New
York 10014, USA. Penguin Books Australia Ltd, Ringwood, Victoria, Australia.
Penguin Books Canada Ltd, 10 Alcorn Avenue, Toronto, Ontario, Canada m4v 3b2.
Penguin Books (NZ) Ltd, 182–190 Wairau Road, Auckland 10, New Zealand
· Penguin Books Ltd, Registered Offices: Harmondsworth, Middlesex, England ·
These extracts have been taken from *Among the Cities* **by Jan Morris,
published by Penguin Books in 1985.** This edition published 1995 · Copyright
© Jan Morris, 1985 · All rights reserved · Filmset by Datix International Limited,
Bungay, Suffolk · Printed in England by Clays Ltd, St Ives plc · Except in the
United States of America, this book is sold subject to the condition that it shall not,
by way of trade or otherwise, be lent, re-sold, hired out, or otherwise circulated
without the publisher's prior consent in any form of binding or cover other than
that in which it is published and without a similar condition including this
condition being imposed on the subsequent purchaser · 10 9 8 7 6 5 4 3 2 1

CONTENTS

The Islanders

MANHATTAN, 1979

Manhattan is always different but always the same — shifting from day to day in fashion, trend or bigotry, constant in the fascination and excitement of its presence. When I went to New York in 1979 to write this essay I had been there every year for twenty-five years — it was my Silver Jubilee of Manhattan: but I found it fresh and fathomless as ever, and went home to Wales, as usual, in a condition of slightly intoxicated, and perceptibly sentimental, enthralment.

Sometimes, from high office windows in Manhattan, you can make out a faint white blob in the green of Central Park far below. It is like the unresolved blur of a nebula in the night sky: and just as through a telescope the fuzz in Andromeda resolves itself into M31, so that whitish object in the park, defined through binoculars, becomes a phenomenon hardly less spectacular. It is the polar bear in the Central Park Zoo, and even as you focus your lenses, bringing his indistinct physique into clarity, with a shaggy shake of his head he swings his great form vigorously from one extremity of his cage to the other. The bear lives alone in his compound down there, and I am told that he is a character of weird and forceful originality — sadly neurotic, some informants suggested, genuinely imaginative, others thought. He is a bear like no other, and it is not the fact of his captivity that makes him so, I am sure, but its remarkable location. Destiny has deposited that animal plumb in the middle of Manhattan: you might say he is the central New Yorker. He affects me profoundly, whenever I see him, and when I put my binoculars down, and only the suggestion of him remains, apparently inanimate among the trees, all around him in my mind's eye the marvellous and terrible island of Manhattan concentrically extends, ring after ring of cage, ditch or rampart, precinct limit and electoral boundary, Hudson, East River and Atlantic itself – the greatest of all the zoos, whose inhabitants prowl up and down, like victims of some terrific spell, for ever and ever within it.

For Manhattan really is an island, even now, separated from the mainland still by a channel just wide enough for the Circle Line boats to continue their pleasure circuits, and it is this condition of enclave that gives the place its sting. Like the bear, its citizens are heightened, one way or another, by their confinement. If they are unhappier than most populaces, they are merrier too. If they are trapped in some ways, they are brilliantly liberated in others. Sometimes their endless pacing to and fro is sad to see, but when the weather is right and the sap is rising, then it assumes an exhilarating rhythm, and the people of Manhattan seem to dance along their avenues, round and round the city squares, in and out the sepulchral subway.

Images of confinement certainly haunt me in Manhattan, but the first thing that always strikes me, when I land once more on the island, is its fearful and mysterious beauty. Other cities have built higher now, or sprawl more boisterously over their landscapes, but there is still nothing like the looming thicket of the Manhattan skyscrapers, jumbled and overbearing. Le Corbusier hated this ill-disciplined spectacle, and conceived his own Radiant City, an antiseptic hybrid of art and ideology, in direct antithesis to it. His ideas, though, mostly bounced off this vast mass of vanity. Tempered though it has been from time to time by zoning law and social trend, Manhattan remains a mammoth mess, a stupendous clashing of light and dark and illusory perspective, splotched here and there by wastelands of slum or demolition, wanly patterned by the grid of its street system, but essentially, whatever the improvers do to it, whatever economy decrees or architectural fashion advises, the supreme monument to that elemental human instinct, Free-For-All.

But the glowering ecstasy of it! No other city, not even Venice, projects for me a more orgasmic kind of allure. I do not mean the popular phallic symbolism of the place, its charged erections thrusting always into the sky. I am thinking of more veiled seductions, the shadows in its deep streets, the watchfulness, the ever-present hint of concealment or allusion. The clarity of Manhattan is what the picture postcards emphasize, but I prefer Manhattan hazed, Manhattan reticent and heavy-eyed.

I like it, for instance, on a very, very hot day, a day when emerging into the streets from the air conditioning is like changing continents. Then a film of chemical vapour seems to drift around the city, fudging every edge, gauzing every vista. Exhausted, half-deserted, the island seems to stand stupefied in the haze: but sometimes flashes of sunlight, piercing the humidity, are reflected momentarily off windows or metal roofs, and then I am reminded of those uncertain but resplendent cities, vaporous but diamond-twinkling, which stand in the backgrounds of all the best fairy tales.

Conversely on a grey lowering day it is like some darkling forest. The tops of the buildings are lost in fog, and only their massive bases, like the trunks of so many gigantic oaks, are to be seen beneath the cloud base. I feel a mushroom feeling in   3

Manhattan then, and the huddled scurry of the people on the sidewalks, the shifting patterns of their umbrellas, the swish of cars through pothole puddles, the blinking of the traffic lights one after another through the slanting rain, the plumes of steam which, like geysers from the subterranean, spout into the streets – all this speaks fancifully to me, here in *urbanissimus*, of clearing, glade and woodland market.

But best of all, for this reluctant and secretive beauty of the island, I like to walk very early in the morning down to Battery Park, the southernmost tip of it, its gazebo on the world, looking out across the great bay towards the Narrows and the open sea. This is a melancholy pleasure, for the shipping which used to make this the busiest basin on earth has mostly been dispersed now. Most of the Atlantic liners sail no more, the freighters mostly berth elsewhere around the bay, and of the myriad public ferries which used to sail like so many water insects to and from Manhattan, only the old faithful to Staten Island survives.

So early in the morning, the scene down at the Battery is not likely to be bustling. If it is misty, it is likely to be a little spooky, in fact. The mist lies heavy over the greyish water, muffled sirens sound, somewhere a sound-buoy intermittently hoots. Perhaps a solitary tanker treads cautiously towards Brooklyn, or a pilot boat, its crew collars-up against the dank, chugs out towards the Narrows. Early commuters emerge blearily from the ferry station; two or three layabouts are stretched on park benches, covered in rags and newspaper; a police car sometimes wanders by, its policemen slumped in their seats dispassionately, like men at the end of a shift.

It seems eerily isolated and exposed, and you feel as though the few of you are all alone, there at the water's edge. But as the morning draws on and the mist clears, something wonderful happens. It is like the printing of a Polaroid picture. The wide sweep of the bay gradually reveals its outlines, the Statue of Liberty appears unforeseen upon her plinth, lesser islands show themselves, and as you turn your back upon the water, glistening now in the freshening breeze, it turns out that the tremendous presence of Manhattan itself, its serried buildings rank on rank, has been looking over your shoulder all the time.

I was walking one day down Sixth Avenue (as New Yorkers still sensibly prefer to call the Avenue of the Americas) when I saw a lady taking a bath, fully clothed, in the pool outside the Time-Life Building. This struck me as a good idea, for it was a hot and sticky day, and I approached her to express my admiration for her initiative. I did not get far. When she saw me step her way she sat bolt upright in the pool, water streaming off her lank hair and down the clinging blue fabric of her dress, and screamed obscenities at me. It was unnerving. Shrill, wild and dreadfully penetrating, her voice pursued me like an eldritch curse, and everyone looked accusingly at me, as though I had insulted the poor soul, and deserved all the imprecations she could command (and her repertoire, I must say, was impressive).

Nobody, I noticed, looked accusingly at *her*. She was evidently mad, and so unaccusable. Confined like that bear on their own rock, the people of Manhattan are the most neurotic community on earth. The twitch, the mutter, the meaningless shriek, the foul-mouthed mumble, the disjointed shuffle – these are native gestures of the island. Pale and ghostly, violently made up or sunk in despair are thousands of its faces – clowns' faces, chalk white and crimson, or haunted faces that have survived concentration camps, or faces alive with a crazy innocence, like those of murderous infants.

Every great city has its bewildered minority – the confused are always with us. Manhattan, though, is the only one I know that sometimes seems on the brink of general nervous breakdown. Intensely clever, cynical, introspective, feverishly tireless, it has all the febrile brightness, alternating with despondency, that sometimes attends insomnia, together with the utter self-absorption of the schizophrenic. Few residents of Manhattan really much care what happens anywhere else. Backs to the sea and the waterways east and west, theirs is a crosstown outlook, focusing ever closer, ever more preoccupied, upon the vortex of the place – which is to say, themselves. 'Does dyslexia,' I heard an interviewer say in all seriousness on television one day, 'crop up in other parts of the country, or is it pertinent only to Manhattan?'

Lord Melbourne, when he was Queen Victoria's Prime Minister, was once asked by an anxious acquaintance for his advice on how best to cope with the problems of life. 'Be easy,' was all the statesman said. 'I like an easy man.' He would have to look hard for one in Manhattan, where the old gamblers' precept 'Let it ride' has long been rejected. Analysis, I sometimes think, is the principal occupation of Manhattan – analysis of trends, analysis of options, analysis of style, analysis of statistics, analysis above all of self. Freud has much to answer for, in this island of tangled dreams, and the women's movement has evidently liberated all too many women only into agonized doubt and self-questioning.

But actually, like most people New Yorkers like to be thought a bit crazy. When they had a poll in New York and Los Angeles, each city complacently claimed its own population to be madder than the other. I know a business corporation in Manhattan – I dare not mention its name – which seems to me to be run entirely, top to bottom, by people off their balance. The minute I enter its offices, an uneasy suggestion of collective haywire assails me. Concealed and unapproachable behind his monumental mahogany doors sits the president of this corporation of nuts, mad as a hatter himself, and in hierarchy of psychosis his subordinates hiss and fiddle their days away below. Sometimes a whole department is fired: sometimes a surprised and hitherto unnoticed employee is plucked from obscurity and made the head of a division for a month or two; sometimes the company, which deals (let us say) in commodity shares, suddenly invests a few million dollars in a Chattanooga umbrella factory, or a grocery chain in Nicaragua.

They have all been driven off their heads, I suppose, by the needling and hallucinatory pressures of Manhattan, the prick of ambition, the fear of failure: and in their eyes I see, as they contemplate the future of their lunatic careers, just the same fierce but loveless passion that one sees in the eyes of brainwashed cultists – a blend of alarm and mindless dedication, dimly tinged with tranquillizers.

I say hallucinatory pressures, because to the outsider there is much to Manhattan that seems surreal. This is not a place of natural fantasy, like Los Angeles – its spirit is fundamentally logical and rationalist, as befits a city of merchants, bankers and stockbrokers. But its daily life is spattered with aspects and episodes of an unhinged sensibility, of which I record here, from a recent two-weeks' stay on the island, a few by no means extraordinary examples:

Item: An eminent, kind and cultivated actress, beautifully dressed, is taking a cab to an address on Second Avenue. Cabdriver: 'Whereabouts is that on Second Avenue, lady?' Actress, without a flicker in her equanimity: 'Don't ask me, bud. You're the fucking cab-driver.'

Item: Sign at a Front Street garage: NO GAS. DEALTH IN FAMILY.

Item: At the headquarters of the New York police, which is at Police Plaza, and is approached along the Avenue of the Finest, there is a functionary called the Chief of Organized Crime. I heard an administrator say to a colleague on the telephone there: 'You're going sick today? Administrative sick or regular sick?'

Item: A young man talks about his experiences in a levitation group: 'Nobody's hovering yet but we're lifting up and down again. We're hopping. I've seen a guy hop fifteen feet from the lotus position, and no one could do that on the level of trying.'

Item: Coming down in the hotel elevator at the New York Hilton is a delegate to the American Urological Association convention. He is on his way to a presentation on Pre-Lymphadenectomy Staging of Testicular Tumours, and his name, I see from his lapel card, is Dr Portnoy.

Item: An aged court-appointed lawyer, down at the state courts, histrionically convinces the judge, with a florid wealth of legal jargon and gesture, that an adjournment is necessary, but spotting a row of hostile witnesses as he passes through the courtroom on his way out, loudly offers them a comment: 'Too bad, assholes.'

Item: Graffito in Washington Square: YIPPIES, JESUS FREAKS AND MOONIES ARE GOVERNMENT OPERATED.

Item: Four angry ladies are trying to enter St Patrick's Cathedral by the wrong entrance for the celebration of the cathedral's centenary, to be attended by three cardinals and eight archbishops. Their way is barred, but as the chanting of the mass sounds through the half-closed door, I hear them responding with a genuine *cri de coeur*: 'We must get in! We must! We're tourists from Israel!'

Item: The terrifyingly ambitious, inexhaustible girl supervisor at one of the downtown McDonalds. Over the serving counter one may see the glazed and vacant faces of the cooks, a black man and a couple of Puerto Ricans, who appear to speak no English: in front of that small tyrant strides peremptorily up and down, yelling orders, angrily correcting errors, and constantly falling back upon an exhortatory slogan of her own: 'C'mon, guys, today guys, today . . .!' The cooks look back in pained incomprehension.

Item: I feel a sort of furry clutch at my right leg, and peering down, find that it is being bitten by a chow. 'Oh, Goochy you naughty thing,' says its owner, who is following behind with a brush and shovel for clearing up its excrement, 'you don't know that person.'

Item: At nine in the morning, on a smart street in the East Seventies, a highly respectable middle-aged lady leans against the hood of a black Mercedes, meditatively scratching her crotch.

Item: It is night, and drizzling. I am crossing Park Avenue on my way home, and looking to my left to the mass of the Grand Central Terminal, see a sort of vision: piled on top of the New York General Building, and silhouetted floodlit against the monstrous Pan Am tower behind, the pinnacled cupola of the structure looks, just for a moment, like a shrine – a stupa, perhaps. I pause in astonishment, half expecting to hear mystical prayer bells sounding, until a passing cab, hooting its horn and showering me with mud from an adjacent gutter, scuttles me back to realism.

How small it is! Thirteen miles long from tip to tip, two and a half miles across at its widest point – at Eighty-sixth Street, I believe. It would be hard to be anonymous for long in Manhattan, if anyone well known ever wanted to be. When I was here last I went to see Mr Woody Allen's masterpiece *Manhattan*, the truest contemporary work of art I know about the island: after the show I went next door for a cup of tea at the Russian Tea Room, and there, large as life, toying with what I assume to have been a blini, was Mr Allen himself.

Sometimes it is hard to remember that this is one of the earth's most powerful cities, for in some ways it is oddly parochial. *The New York Times* is half a newspaper of international record, and half a parish magazine, with full obituaries of respected local insurance managers, and blow-by-blow accounts of the engagement of Miss Henrietta Zlyman to Edward Twistletoe III. Like all great metropolises, Manhattan is divided into lesser enclaves, each with its own personality and purpose, but the skinny shape of the island, the rigidity of its grid and the flatness of it all, make it impossible for any district to feel remote from any other. You can easily walk from Central Park to Battery Park in a gentle morning stroll; I boarded a bus recently with an acquaintance in the very heart of Harlem, all dingy tenements and apparently abandoned stores, and before he had finished telling me his war experiences we had arrived outside the Plaza Hotel. Besides, the great landmarks of the place, the Empire State Building, the twin towers of the World Trade Center, are so enormous that they are visible almost everywhere, and give the island a foreshortened sort of intimacy.

All crammed in like this, it is no wonder that the inhabitants of Manhattan sway to and fro, as though with minds linked, to the shifting tunes of fashion. No city in the world, I think, is so subject to the *diktats* of critics, snobs and arbiters of taste. Manhattan feeds upon itself – intravenously, perhaps. A very public elite dominates its gossip columns and décors, the same faces over and over, seen at the same currently fashionable clubs and restaurants, Stork Club in one generation, Studio 54 another, drinking the statutory drinks, *kir* yesterday, Perrier today, using the same ephemeral 'in' words – when I was here last, for example, 'schlep', 'supportive', 'copacetic', 'significant others'.

I was taken one evening, at my own request, to the saloon currently the trendiest in town, Elaine's on Second Avenue. Everyone knows Elaine's. Secretaries hang about its bar, in the hope of being adopted by wild celebrities, young executives talk about it the morning after, and even the most intelligent of public people, it seems, literate directors and scholarly critics, unaccountably think it worth while to be seen there. No such phenomenon exists in Europe, for Elaine's is neither very expensive nor exactly exclusive – anyone can go and prop up the bar. I detested it, though: the noise, the jam-packed tables, the showing-off, the gush, the unwritten protocol which gives the best-known faces the most prominent tables, and banishes unknowns to the room next door. The beautiful people looked less than beautiful shouting their heads off in the din. The waiter resisted my attempts to have scampis without garlic (not liking garlic is *infra dig* in Manhattan).

I felt fascinated and appalled, both at the same time: but more surprising, I felt a bit patronizing – for all of a sudden, as I observed those bobbing faces there, wreathed in display or goggled in sycophancy, fresh as I was from my little village on the north-west coast of Wales, I felt myself to be among provincials.

Not a sensation I often get in New York. More often, when I am at large in this incomparable city, I feel myself to be among ultimates. *How're they gonna get me back on the farm?* This is, after all, The City of our times, as Rome was in classical days, as Constantinople was through centuries of Mediterranean history. This is everyone's metropolis, for there is no nation that has not contributed something to Manhattan, if only a turn of phrase or a category of bun. I went one day to the street festival which is held each May on Ninth Avenue, one of the most vividly cosmopolitan thoroughfares on the island, and realized almost too piquantly what it means to be a city of all peoples: smell clashing with smell, from a mile of sidewalk food stalls, sesame oil at odds with curry powder, Arabic drifting into Ukrainian among the almost impenetrable crowds, Yiddish colliding with Portuguese, and all the way down the avenue the discordant blending of folk-music, be it from Polish flageolet, Mexican harmonica or balalaika from Sofia.

Nothing provincial there! And if over the past 300 years the clambering upon this huge raft of refugees, adventurers, idealists and crooks from every land has given Manhattan always a quality of paradigm or fulcrum, so when it comes to the end of the world, I think, most people can most easily imagine the cataclysm in the context of this island. The great towers crumpling and sagging into themselves, the fires raging up the ravaged boulevards, the panicked rush of the people, like rats or lemmings, desperately into the boiling water – these are twentieth-century man's standard images of Doomsday: and in my own view, if God is truly going to sit one day in judgement upon the doings of mankind, he is likely to set up court on the corner of Broadway and Forty-second Street, where he can deal first (and leniently I am sure) with the purveyors of Sextacular Acts Live on Stage.

We live in baleful times, and it is a pity that Manhattan, that temple of human hope and ingenuity, should be obliged to fill this particular role of parable. There is no denying, though, that there often passes across the face of this city, like a shudder, a sense of ominous portent. I read one morning in the *Times* that a woman, walking the previous day down a street near City Hall, had been attacked by a pack of rats 'as big as rabbits'. I leapt into a cab at once, but Manhattan had beaten me to it: already a small crowd was peering with evident satisfaction into the festering abandoned lot from which the rodents had sprung. Already one of your archetypal New Yorkers had appointed himself resident expert, and was pointing out to enthralled office workers one of your actual rats, *almost* as big as a rabbit, which was sitting morosely in a wire trap among the piled rubbish. What became of the original victim, I asked? 'I guess she was some kind of screwball. She just drove off screaming . . .'

I would have driven off screaming too, if those rabbit-rats had attached themselves to me, but around the corner, almost within excretion distance of the rat pit, business was brisk as ever at the neighbourhood takeout food store. New Yorkers are hardened to horror, I suppose, and perhaps it is this acclimatization that gives their island its sense of fated obliteration. It might be designed for nemesis, and suggests to me sometimes an amphitheatre of pagan times, in which ladies and rats, like gladiators and wild beasts, are pitted against each other for the rude entertainment of the gods.

Everything comes on to the island: nothing much goes off, even by evaporation. Once it was a gateway to a New World, now it is a portal chiefly to itself. Manhattan long ago abandoned its melting-pot function. Nobody even tries to Americanize the Lebanese or the Lithuanians now, and indeed the ethnic enclaves of the island seem to me to become more potently ethnic each time I visit the place. Nothing could be much more Italian than the Festival of St Anthony of Padua down on Mulberry Street, when the families of Little Italy stroll here and there through their estate, pausing often to greet volatile contemporaries and sometimes munching the soft-shelled crabs which, spread-eagled on slices of bread like zoological specimens, are offered loudly for sale by street vendors. Harlem has become almost a private city in itself, no longer to be slummed through by whities after dinner, while Manhattan's Chinatown is as good a place as anywhere in the world to test your skill at that universal challenge, trying to make a Chinese waiter smile.

So the lights blaze down fiercely upon a tumultuous arena: but its millions of gladiators (and wild beasts) are not in the least disconcerted by the glare of it, or daunted by the symbolic battles in which they are engaged, but are concerned chiefly to have swords of the fashionable length, to be seen to advantage from the more expensive seats, and preferably to face the lions at the same time as Jackie Onassis, say, or Dick Cavett if you like.

Back to the park. At the centre of the world's present preoccupation with Manhattan, for one reason and another, stands Central Park. 'Don't go walking in that Park,' they will warn you from China to Peru, or 'Tell me frankly,' they ask, 'is it true what they say about Central Park?'

The Park is the centre of the island too, no man's land amid the surrounding conflict of masonry – on the postal map it forms a big oblong blank, the only portion of Manhattan without a zip code. To the north is Harlem, to the south is Rockefeller Center, on one flank is the opulence of the Upper East Side, to the west are the newly burgeoning streets that sprout, teeming with artists, agents, Polish grocers and music students, right and left off Columbus Avenue. It is like a big rectangular scoop in the city, shovelled out and stacked with green. It covers 840 acres, and it is almost everything, to my mind, that a park should not be.

This is a heretical view. Central Park is enormously admired by specialists in planning and urban design. The architectural critic of *The New York Times* calls it the city's greatest single work of architecture. It was laid out in 1856 by Frederick Law Olmsted and Calvert Vaux, and ever since everybody has been saying how marvellous it is. 'One of the most beautiful parks in the world,' thought Baedeker, 1904. 'This great work of art,' says the AIA *Guide to New York City, 1978.*

Not me. With its gloomy hillocks obstructing the view, with its threadbare and desolate prairies, with its consciously contrived variety of landscapes, with its baleful lake and brownish foliage, with the sickly carillon which, hourly from the gates of its appalling zoo, reminds me horribly of the memorial chimes at Hiroshima, Central Park seems to me the very antithesis of the fresh and natural open space, the slice of countryside, that a city park should ideally be.

Nevertheless the world is right when, invited to think of Manhattan, it is likely to think first these days of Central Park. If I deny its ethereal beauty, I do not for a moment dispute its interest. It is one of the most interesting places on earth. 'It is inadvisable,' warns the Michelin guide, 1968, 'to wander alone through the more deserted parts of the park': but wandering alone nevertheless through this extraordinary retreat, dominated on all sides by the towering cliffs of Manhattan, is to enjoy one of the greatest of all human shows, in perpetual performance from dawn through midnight.

You want tradition? There go the lumbering barouches, their horse smells hanging pungent in the air long after they have left their stands outside the Plaza, their Dutch trade delegates, their Urological Association conventioneers, or even their honeymooners from Iowa, somewhat self-consciously sunk in their cushions, and their coachmen leaning back, as they have leant for a century or more, whip in hand to ask their customers where they're from.

You want irony? Consider the layabouts encouched apparently permanently on their benches along the East Side, beyond the open-air book-stalls, prickly and raggedy, bony and malodorous, camped there almost in the shadow of the sumptuous Fifth Avenue apartment houses, and more tellingly still perhaps, actually within earshot of the feebly growling lions, the cackling birds and funereal carillon of the zoo.

You want vaudeville? Try the joggers on their daily exercise. Doggedly they lope in their hundreds around the ring road, generally cleared of traffic on their behalf, like migrating animals homed in upon some inexplicable instinct, or numbed survivors from some catastrophe out of sight. Some are worn lean as rakes by their addiction, some drop the sweat of repentant obesity. Some flap with huge ungainly breasts. Some tread with a predatory menace, wolflike in the half-hour before they must present that memo about ongoing supportive expenditures to Mr Cawkwell at the office. Sometimes you may hear snatches of very Manhattan conversations, as the enthusiasts labour by – 'So you're saying (gasp) that since 1951 (pant) there's been no meaningful change whatever (puff) in our society?' Sometimes you may observe a jogger who has taken his dog with him on a leash, and who, obliged to pause while the animal defecates behind a bush, compromises by maintaining a standing run, on the spot, looking consequently for all the world as though he is dying for a pee himself.

But no, it is the sinister you want, isn't it? 'It is inadvisable to wander alone, despite the frequent police patrols on horseback or by car . . .' That is what Central Park is most famous for these days, and it is not hard to find. I have never been mugged in Central Park, never seen anyone else harmed either, but I have had my chill moments all the same. More than once, even as the joggers pad around their circuit, I have noticed perched distantly on the rocky outcrops which protrude among the dusty trees, groups of three or four youths, silently and thoughtfully watching. They wear dark glasses, as likely as not, and big floppy hats, and they recline upon their rock in attitudes of mocking but stealthy grace, motionless, as though they were fingering their flick-knives.

I waved to one such group of watchers once, as I walked nervously by: but they responded only by looking at each other in a bewildered way, and shifting their long legs a trifle uneasily upon the stone.

All around the city roars. Well, no, not roars – buzzes, perhaps. The energy of Manhattan is less leonine than waspish, and its concerns are, for so tremendous a metropolis, wonderfully individual and idiosyncratic. Despite appearances, Manhattan is an especially human city, where personal aspirations, for better or for worse, unexpectedly take priority.

Perhaps this is because, unlike either of the other global cities (for in my view there are only two, Paris and London) – unlike its peers, New York is not a capital. True, the headquarters of the United Nations is down by the East River, but architecturally it is the perfect reflection of its lacklustre political self, and one hardly notices it. True too that the municipal affairs of this city, 17 being on so momentous a scale, are equivalent I suppose to the entire political goings-on of many lesser republics. But it is not really a political city. Affairs of state and patriotism rarely intrude. Even the state capital is far away in Albany, and Manhattan conversations do not often turn to infighting within the Democratic Party, or the prospects of Salt III.

There is not much industry on the island, either, in any sociological or aesthetic sense: few blue-collared workers making for home with their lunch boxes, few manufacturing plants to belch their smoke into the Manhattan sky. This is a city of more intricate concerns, a city of speculators and advisers, agents and middlemen and sorters-out and go-betweens. Many of the world's most potent corporations have their headquarters here, but their labour forces are mostly conveniently far away. Fortunes are made here, and reputations, not steel ingots or automobiles.

The pace of New York is legendary, but nowadays in my opinion illusory. Businessmen work no harder, no faster, than in most other great cities. But New Yorkers spend so much time contemplating their personal affairs, analysing themselves, examining their own reactions, that the time left for business is necessarily rushed. Do not suppose, when the Vice-President of Automated Commercial leaves his office in such a hurry, that he is meeting the Overseas Sales Director of Toyuki Industries: good gracious no, he is leaving early because he simply must have it out face to face with Brian about his disgraceful behaviour with that Edgar person in the disco last night.

More than any other place I know, to do business in New York you must understand your colleagues' circumstances. They often need worrying out. There are some tell-tale signs indeed, like tribal tattoos – short hair for Brian and Edgar, for example, droopy moustaches and canvas shoes for aspirant literary men, rasping voices and nasal intonations for girls who hope to get into television, hands in trouser pockets for Ivy League executives. But you should take no chances. The tangles of Manhattan marital and emotional life, which provide inexhaustible hours of instruction to the social observer, set the tone of this place far more than torts, share prices or bills of lading.

There is hardly a citizen of Manhattan, of any race, creed or social class, who does not have some fascinating emotional imbroglio to relate – and hardly a citizen, either, who fails to relate it. Nitter-natter, chit-chat, *you would hardly believe it, so I said never, so she said absolutely* – sibilantly across this city of gossip, from Wall Street clubs to bars of Harlem one seems to hear the tide of confession and confidence, unremitting as the flood of the traffic, rattly as the clang of the subway trains which now and then emerges from grilles beneath one's feet.

Is this inbreeding? Certainly there is something perceptibly incestuous about Manhattan, now that the diversifying flow of immigration has abated. This is no longer the lusty stud of the world. Ellis Island, through whose lugubrious halls so many millions of newcomers passed into the land of fertility, is only a museum now, and ethnically Manhattan has lost its virile momentum. You feel the migratory thrust far more vividly in Toronto, and most of New York's contemporary immigrants are hardly immigrants at all, in the old risk-all kind, but are Puerto Ricans joining their relatives, or Colombians cooperatively financed by the drug-rings of Jackson Heights.

They are seldom inspired, as their predecessors were, by any flaming spirit of release or dedication, and they very soon fall into the Manhattan mode. 'Well it's like I say, see, I got this lady I used to know back in Bogotá. She says to me, "Leon," she says, "I wantya to know, I'm fond of you, truly I am, but there's this problem of Juan's baby, see?" "To hell with Juan's baby," I says, "what's Juan's baby to me?" And she says, "Leon, honey," she says, "listen to me . . ."'"

'Give me your tired, your poor, your huddled masses yearning to breathe free . . .' An occasional Russian dissident appears in New York these days, to endure his statutory press conference before being whisked away to CIA debriefing or associate professorship somewhere. But the loss of the grand old purpose, so stoutly declaimed by the Lady of Liberty out there in the bay, means that Manhattan is recognizably past its prime.

Every city has its heyday, the moment when its purpose is fulfilled and its spirit bursts into full flower, and Manhattan's occurred I think in the years between the Great Depression, when the indigents squatted in Central Park, and the end of the Second World War, when the GIs returned in splendour as the saviours of liberty. In those magnificent years this small island, no more than a fantastic dream to most of the peoples of the world, stood everywhere for the fresh start and the soaring conception. Manhattan was Fred Astaire and the sun-topped Chrysler Building! Manhattan was the Jeep and Robert Benchley! Manhattan was rags-to-riches, free speech, Mayor La Guardia and the Rockettes!

No wonder nostalgia booms on Broadway. Those were the days of the American innocence, before responsibility set in, and every dry and racy old song of the period, every new Art Deco furniture boutique, is an expression of regret. European Powers pine for their lost glories with bearskin parades or jangling cavalry: New York looks back with *Ain't Misbehavin'*, or the refurbishing, just as it was, of that prodigy of Manhattan gusto,

Radio City Music Hall (whose designer reportedly had ozone driven through its ventilator shafts, to keep its audiences festive, and toyed with the idea of laughing gas too . . .). Fortunately the old days come quickly in a city that is not yet 300 years old, and the authentic bitter-sweetness is relatively easy to achieve. I was touched myself by the furnishing of a restaurant equipped entirely with the fittings of one of the old Atlantic liners, those dowagers of the Manhattan piers, until I discovered that the ship concerned was the *Caronia*, whose launching I remember as clear as yesterday.

The memories of that time are legendary already, and moving fast into myth. Nothing in travel stirs me more than the dream of that old Manhattan, the Titan City of my childhood, when the flamboyant skyscrapers soared one after the other into the empyrean, when John D. Rockefeller, Jr., pored over the plans for his Center like a modern Midas, when the great liners stalked through the bay with their complements of celebrities and ship-board reporters, and the irrepressible immigrants toiled and clawed their way up the line of Manhattan, from Ellis Island to the Lower East Side to the Midtown affluence of their aspirations. Its monuments are mostly there to see still, newly fashionable as the buildings of the day-before-yesterday are apt to become, and sometimes even now you may stumble across one of its success stories: the waiter proudly boasting that, since arriving penniless and friendless from Poland, he has never been out of work for a day – the famous publisher, in the penthouse suite of his own skyscraper, whose mother landed in Manhattan with a placard around her neck, announcing her name, trade and language.

Rockefeller Center is the theatre of this mood. Raymond

Hood, the creator of its central structure, the RCA Building, was reminded one day that he had come to Manhattan in the first place with the declared intention of becoming the greatest architect in New York. 'So I did,' he responded, looking out of the window at that stupendous thing, jagged and commanding high above, 'and by God, so I am!' The magnificent brag, the revelatory vision, the ruthless opportunism, the limitless resource – these were the attributes of Rockefeller Center, as of Manhattan, in the heady years of its construction: and when at winter time they turn the sunken café into an ice rink, then in the easy delight of the skaters under the floodlights, some so hilariously inept, some so showily skilful, with the indulgent crowd leaning over the railings to watch, and the waltz music only half drowned by the city's rumble – then I sometimes seem to be, even now, back in those boundless years of certainty.

If the conviction is lost, the abilities remain. This is the most gifted of all the human settlements of the earth, and there are moments in Manhattan when the sheer talent of the place much moves me. I happened to be in the Pan Am Building recently when an orchestra of young people was giving a lunch-time concert in the central concourse. This is a common enough event in Manhattan, a place of inescapable music, but somehow it seized my imagination and twisted my emotions. No other city, I swear, could provide an interlude so consoling. The brilliant young players were so full of exuberance. The audience listened to their Brahms and Vivaldi with such sweet attention. The music sounded wonderfully tender in the heart of all that stone and steel, and seemed to float like a tempering agent down the escalators, through the bland air-conditioned offices, of that

great tower of materialism. ('How beautifully they play,' I remarked in my delight to a man listening beside me, but in the Manhattan manner he brought me harshly down to earth. 'They gotta play beautifully,' he replied. 'Think of the competition.')

The cities of Europe have mostly lost their artists' quarters, swallowed up now in housing estates or ripped apart by ring roads. In Manhattan, Bohemia flourishes still, in many an eager alcove. This is a city of the streets and cafés, where human contact, carnal or platonic, is still easy to arrange, where no young artist need feel alone or benighted for long, and where no ambition is too extravagant. Manhattan probably has more than its fair share of artistic phonies, and SoHo, currently the most popular painters' quarter, certainly exhibits an adequate proportion of junkyard collages or knobs of inadequately sandpapered walnut labelled 'Significant Others 3'. But tucked away in the attics, cheap hotels, apartment blocks and converted brownstones of this island a myriad genuine artists and craftsmen are at work, impervious to trend and disdainful of sham.

I like to spend Sunday mornings watching the alfresco circus down at Washington Square, the gateway to Greenwich Village, where wandering musicians and amateur jugglers compete for the attention of the sightseers with virtuoso frisbee throwers, classical in their skills and gestures, impromptu demagogues, chess players, itinerant idiots and Rastafari bravos. Often and again then, when I am sitting on my park bench watching this colourful world go by, I spot a fellow practitioner of my craft, alone on *his* bench with *his* notebook, and as our eyes meet I wonder if I ought to feel compassion for him, as the struggling artist from his austere garret somewhere, or envy, as the author of tomorrow's runaway bestseller.

Contrary to the world's conceptions, New York is rich in people of integrity. In a city of such attainments it has to be so.

23

This is a city of dedicated poets, earnest actors and endlessly rehearsing musicians. Draft after draft its writers are rejecting, and there are more good pianists playing in New York every evening than in the whole of Europe – smouldering jazz pianists in the downtown clubs, crazy punk pianists on Bleecker Street, stuffed-shirt romantic pianists in the Midtown tourist spots ('Would you mind lowering your voice to a whisper, please, during Mr Maloney's renditioning?'), smashing student pianists practising for next year's Tchaikovsky competition, jolly young pianists accompanying off-Broadway musicals, drop-out pianists, drunk ruined pianists, mendicant pianists with instruments on trolley wheels, Steinway pianists flown by Concorde that afternoon for their concerti at Lincoln Center.

So I am never really deluded by the charlatan inanities of New York. I disregard the fatuous interviewers and repellent respondents of what we are gruesomely encouraged to think of as NBC's Today Family. I sneer not at the sellers of Instant Ginseng. I am not deceived by the coarse-grained editors, hag-ridden by their own accountants, or the ghastly company of celebrities. 'Creativity' is so degraded a word in Manhattan that I hesitate to use it, loathing its translation into salesmen's acuity or publicity gimmick. But creative this place truly is: not in the old audacious style perhaps, but in the quieter, introspective, muddled but honest way that is more the Manhattan manner now.

It would seem inconceivable to Hood or John D., Jr., let alone Commodore Vanderbilt or Pierpont Morgan, but actually in 1979 Manhattan feels a little old-fashioned. The Titan City has come to terms, and recognizes that everything is *not* possible after all. They build more thrilling buildings in Chicago now. They do more astonishing things in Houston. There are more aggressive entrepreneurs in Tokyo or Frankfurt. It is no good coming to Manhattan for the shape of things to come: Singapore or São Paulo might be more reliable guides. In the days of the Great Vision the New Yorkers built an airship mast on the top of the Empire State Building almost as a matter of course, sure that the latest and greatest dirigibles would head straight for Manhattan: it was years, though, before New York was reluctantly persuaded, in our own time, to allow supersonic aircraft to land at JFK.

Manhattan is no longer the fastest, the most daring or even I dare say the richest. For a symbol of its civic energies now, I recommend an inspection of the abandoned West Side Highway, the victim of seven years' municipal indecision, which staggers crumbling on its struts above a wilderness of empty lots, truck parks and shattered warehouses, the only signs of enterprise being the cyclists who cheerfully trundle along the top of it, and the railway coaches of the Ringling Bros., Barnum and Bailey Circus which park themselves habitually underneath.

The falter came, I believe, in the fifties and sixties, when Manhattan began to see *laissez-faire*, perhaps, as a less than absolute ideology. Doubts crept in. The pace slowed a bit. The sense of movement lagged. All the great ships no longer came in their grandeur to the Manhattan piers; the New York airports were far from the island; today even the helicopters, which were for a couple of decades the lively familiars of Manhattan, are banned from their wayward and fanciful antics around the skyscrapers. Bauhaus frowned down upon Radio City Music Hall, in those after-the-glory years, and most of Manhattan's mid-century architecture was, by Hood's standards, timid and banal. The truly original buildings were few, and worse still for my taste, the swagger-buildings were not built at all.

25

When, in the early 1970s, the World Trade Center was erected in a late spasm of the old hubris – the two tallest towers on earth then, beckoning once more the world across the bay – all Manhattan groaned at the change in its familiar skyline, and to this day it is hard to find a New Yorker willing to admit to admiration for that arrogant pair of pylons. The fashionable philosophy of smallness strongly appealed to New Yorkers, in their new mood of restraint, and nowadays when citizens want to show you some innovation they are proud of, they generally take you to a dainty little kerbside park with waterfalls, or Roosevelt Island, an itsy-bitsy enclave of sociological good taste. Suavity, discretion and even modesty are the architectural qualities admired in Manhattan now, and the colossal is no longer welcomed.

And believe it or not, *quaintness* approaches. Mr Philip Johnson's latest building is to be crowned with a decorative device like the back of a Chesterfield sofa: so does old age creep up, all but unsuspected, upon even the most dynamic organisms – Time's A-Train, hurrying near! Manhattan is no longer critical in the atomic sense: 'No Nukes' is a proper slogan for this gently decelerating powerhouse.

It is not a sad spectacle. I find it endearing. If New York has lost the power to amaze, it is gaining the power to charm. They did not mean it seriously, when they called this Little Old New York, but the phrase is losing its irony now. Old Manhattan inevitably becomes – small geographically it always was – little and old in the figurative sense, in the cosy familiar endearing sense. Manhattan telephone operators, who used to be mere human mechanisms, call one 'dear' nowadays: and at the New York Hilton, that very shrine of impersonal efficiency, there is somebody down in the kitchens who actually recognizes my voice, every time I go there, and sends me up my breakfast with kind endearment and inquiries after my family.

It happened that when I was in Manhattan, Bonwit Teller, for generations one of the smartest stores on Fifth Avenue, closed its doors to make way for a building development. I went along there on the last day, and what a sentimental journey that was! Tears came to saleswomen's eyes, as they pottered for the last time along the atrocious hats, unsellable ceramics, belts and bent coat hangers which were all that remained of their once delectable stock: and an elderly customer I buttonholed by the elevators seemed almost distraught – something beautiful was going out of her life, she said, 'a bit of New York, a little bit of me'.

Bonwit's was quick to remind us, in the next day's *New York Times*, that they have plenty of stores elsewhere, but still the event really did touch some heart-chords in New York. Sentimentality, eccentricity, Earl Grey tea – all these are signs of a society growing old, but doing it, on the whole, gracefully. There is much that is jaded or curdled, of course, to the culture of Little Old New York. Violence really is a curse of the place, circumscribing the lives of hundreds of thousands of people, and blighting whole districts of the city – when the donor of the East River Fountain was asked why it had not been spouting recently, he said he assumed it was clogged with corpses. More people in Manhattan, as it happens, suffer from human bites than from rat bites – 764 recorded in 1978, as against 201 from the rats.

Yet I am of the opinion all the same that Manhattan, whose very name is a byword for the mugging, the fast practice, the impossible pressure and the unacceptable vice, has become in its maturity the most truly civilized of the earth's cities. It is where mankind has, for good or for bad, advanced furthest on its erratic course through history, and in unexpected places, in unforeseen situations, its mellowness shows.

I spent a few hours one night with a squad car of the Fifth Precinct, operating out of Elizabeth Street on the Lower East Side, and found it, to my astonishment, a curiously gentlemanly exercise. I am not overfond of policemen as a breed, and have heard the worst about New York's Finest, but I can only report that my experiences that night were altogether disarming.

My pair of cops were textbook, almost comic-book, figures: burly fellows as you would expect, bulging slightly at the belt, with guns sagging heavy at their hips and that peculiar akimbo sort of gait, as though they are about to enter a Japanese wrestling bout, which is peculiar to American policemen. Our calls too were as you might foresee; a potential suicide on the Brooklyn Bridge, some kids starting a fire, a molester in a tenement house, an elderly householder shot through the head by a thirteen-year-old robber. We progressed around town, within limits as closely defined as a fox's hunting territory, with the proper alternation of creep and crash, now nosing insidiously into back alleys, where the junkies stared blankly at our passing, now switching our yelper on and exploding through the traffic in our battered sedan as though wild horses were carrying us.

But I was surprised, whenever we got there, by the moderation of these Fifth Precinct heavies. I have ridden with big-city policemen in many countries, Bolivia to Hong Kong, and these fellows seemed to me the nearest of them all to the neighbour-hood cops of long ago. The Brooklyn jumper turned out to be a merry fellow, brandishing a bunch of flowers above his head, who said he was merely responding to the Challenge of the Waters, and was given a lift to somewhere less stimulating. The kids were putting out their fire by the time we reached them, and we did not interfere. At the scene of the shooting the local population of Puerto Ricans, Italians and Colombians, far from melting into the night when we and eight other police cars appeared helter-skelter on the scene, howling and flashing, crowded seriously around to help, and were treated I thought with rough but sensible courtesy.

A lucky night? Untypical cops? Perhaps, but nevertheless my night down at the Fifth Precinct, cruising from Chinatown to Mafialand, from Ratner's restaurant still aglow to the seafood joint where they show the bullet holes that killed a Godfather seven years ago – my night down there left me indefinably beguiled and conciliated by Manhattan. I stopped off at an all-night café on my way uptown, and had a pancake. There were a couple of grotesquely painted old ladies in there, looking as though the funeral parlour cosmetician had prematurely had a go at them, and a slob distastefully wiping the last of the egg off his plate with a piece of greasy bread, and two or three night-workers mildly chatting up the waitress, and an obvious English-man, in a striped tie, grinning and bearing it through the jet lag, the time change and the behaviour patterns of the Manhattan midnight.

They used to say of it that it would be a fine place when it was finished. I think in essentials they have completed it now. They are no longer tearing down its buildings, and throwing up new ones, with the fury of their youth. Whole districts are no longer changing character year by year under the impact of the immig-rants. Manhattan has jelled, I think. A feeling not of complacency but perhaps of wry experience pervades Little Old New York now: when, in the Russian Tea Room that day, I caught the eye of Mr Allen, truly the laureate of Manhattan in its silver age, his expression was nothing if not *wistful*.

Actually it is Woody Allen, not that bear, who should be encaged in Central Park, to stand as a focal symbol for peregrinating Welsh essayists. But let me end anyway with one more visit to the Park, that zipless blank at the heart of Manhattan, for a lyrical *envoi* to this piece. I chanced one day, off the joggers' circuit, to come across a young black man fast asleep upon a bench below the lake. His overcoat was thrown over him, his boots were placed neatly side by side upon the ground. His head upon his clasped hands, as in kindergarten plays, he was breathing regularly and gently, as though bewitched.

Even as I watched a grey squirrel, skipping across the green, leapt across his legs to the back of the bench, where it sat tremulously chewing, as squirrels do: and suddenly, almost at the same time, there arose one of those brisk gusts of wind, tangy with salt, which now and then blow a breath of the ocean invigoratingly through New York.

A scatter of leaves and fallen blossoms came with it, flicked and eddied about the bench. The squirrel paused, twitched again and vanished. The black man opened his eyes, as the breeze dusted his face, and seeing me standing there bemused smiled me a slow sleepy smile. 'Be not afeared,' I said ridiculously, on the spur of the moment, 'the isle is full of noises.'

'Yeah,' the man replied, stretching and scratching mightily in the morning. 'Bugs, too.'

Mrs Gupta Never Rang

DELHI, 1975

Indira Gandhi was in power in Delhi in 1975, but though she had clamped the country under a State of Emergency, harshly limiting the press and imprisoning much of the opposition, to the stranger the Indian capital felt much the same as ever. There is not much in this essay to reveal which particular regime governed India at the time of its writing: Delhi is one of those cities whose age, manner and disposition easily absorb the styles of its successive rulers.

'You see,' said the government spokesman, 'you may liken Delhi to the River Ganges, it twists and turns, many other streams join it, it divides into many parts, and it flows into the sea in so many channels that nobody may know which is the true river. You follow my train of thought? It is a metaphysical matter, perhaps. You will do best to burrow under the surface of things and discover what is not revealed to us ordinary mortals! In the meantime, you will take a cup of tea, I hope?' I took a cup of tea, milkless, very sweet, brought by a shuffling messenger in a high-buttoned jacket with a scarf around his neck, and between pleasantries I pondered the spokesman's advice. Indians, of course, love to reduce the prosaic to the mystic. It is part of their Timeless Wisdom. For several centuries the tendency has variously baffled, infuriated, amused and entranced travellers from the West, and India is full of pilgrims still, come from afar to worship at the shrines of insight. But *Delhi*? Delhi is not just a national capital, it is one of the political ultimates, one of the

31

prime movers. It was born to power, war and glory. It rose to greatness not because holy men saw visions there but because it commanded the strategic routes from the North-west, where the conquerors came from, into the rich flatlands of the Ganges delta. Delhi is a soldiers' town, a politicians' town, a journalists', diplomats' town. It is Asia's Washington, though not so picturesque, and lives by ambition, rivalry and opportunism.

'Ah yes,' he said, 'what you are thinking is quite true, but that is the *surface* of Delhi. You are an artist, I know, you should look *beyond*! And if there is anything we can do to help your inquiries,' he added with an engaging waggle of his head, 'you have only to let us know. You may telephone us at any time and we will ring you back with the requisite information in a moment or two. We are here to help! That is why we are here! No, no, that is our duty!'

Certainly Delhi is unimaginably antique, and age is a metaphysic, I suppose. Illustrations of mortality are inescapable there, and do give the place a sort of nagging symbolism. Tombs of emperors stand beside traffic junctions, forgotten fortresses command suburbs, the titles of lost dynasties are woven into the vernacular, if only as street names.

One of the oldest and deadest places I know, for a start, is the crumbled fortress-capital of Tughluqabad in the city's southern outskirts. For a single decade it was a place of terrific consequence, for nearly seven centuries since it has been a grey wasteland of piled stones and ruined alleyways, a *memento mori* by any standard, inhabited only by the disagreeable monkeys which are the familiars of Delhi, and by a melancholy watchman who, recently transferred by the Archaeological Survey from some more frequented historical monument, now sees nobody but the apes from one day to the next.

Or consider, in another kind of allegory, the Lodi Gardens. These are popular promenades, but they are also the cemetery of the Lodi kings who thrived in the early sixteenth century. Here death and life consort on familiar terms, and especially in the early morning, when Delhi people go out for some fresh air before the sun comes up, they offer some piquant juxtapositions. All among the memorials the citizens besport themselves, pursuing their Yogic meditations in the tomb of Sikander Lodi, jogtrotting among the funerary domes, exercising their pampered dachshunds beside the Bara Gumbad Mosque or pissing, in the inescapable Delhi manner, behind the mausoleum of Mohammed Shah.

They used to say, to express the marvellous continuity of Delhi, that seven successive capitals existed here, each superimposed upon the last. Nowadays they are always finding new ones, and the latest tally seems to be fourteen. Few foreigners and still fewer Indians have ever heard of most of the dynasties represented, but here and there across the capital some of them have left not merely tombs or ruins but living remnants of themselves. Embedded, for instance, in one of Delhi's smarter quarters, almost within sight of the Oberoi Intercontinental, is the Moslem village shrine of Nizamuddin, built in the time of the fourteenth-century Sultan Ghiyasuddin Tughluq and still as holy as ever.

Through tortuous mucky lanes one approaches it from the busy highway, past the statutory Indian lines of beggars, crones and saddhus, through the spittle-stained portals where the old men stare, and into the intricate jumble of courts, tombs and arcades that surrounds the mosque of Nizamuddin and its sacred pool. Here mendicants lope around on knobbly staves, saintly 33 scholars are at their books, sweet old ladies sit outside tombs (they are not allowed in, being female), and in the mosque there hustles and brushes the muezzin, an indefatigable goblin figure with white eyebrows and dainty tread. Nothing here is unpremeditated. All moves, though you might not guess it, to an immemorial schedule: the prayer call comes precisely to time, the rituals are meticulously ordered, even the whining beggars have their appointed place in the hierarchy, and when I left the precincts the imam gave me his visiting card – his name is Al Haj Hazrat Peer Qazi Syed Safdar Ali Nizami, and his cable address is HEADPRIEST DELHI.

Even more a living relic, so to speak, is the Begum Timur Jehan Shahzadi of Darya Ganj, in the old walled city of Delhi. This lady is a Moghul princess of the dynasty which made Delhi its capital in the seventeenth century and built the very city, Shahjehanabad, in whose labyrinthine recesses she lives now. Just go to the Old City, her son-in-law had assured me, and ask for the Begum Jehan's house: and though in the event this proved insufficient advice, and I spent half an afternoon stumbling through the high-walled maze of Shahjehanabad, vainly presenting the inquiry, still I relished the form of it, and thought it was rather like knocking on the door of the Great Pyramid, asking for Cheops.

I found her in the end anyway, ensconced in her front sitting-room between portraits of her imperial forebears: a short, decisive old lady with a brief mischievous smile and an air of totally liberated self-possession. There is no pretending that this princess lives much like a princess. Her old house, into which her family moved when they were ejected by later conquerors from their imperial palace, is a beguiling shambles in the old Islamic style: a couple of rooms in the Western manner for the convenience of visitors, the rest more or less medieval – a wide decrepit courtyard, a dusty trellised vine, thickly populated chambers all around. There are granddaughters and sons-in-law and undefined connections; there are skivvies and laundrymen and assorted sweepers; there are children and dogs and unexplained loiterers in doorways. Forty or fifty souls constitute the tumbled court of the Begum Timur Jehan, and through it she moves commandingly in green trousers, issuing instructions, reminiscing about emperors, traitors or ladies of the harem, and frequently consulting her highly organized notebook, all asterisks and cross-references, for addresses or reminders.

Like HEADPRIEST DELHI she lives very near the earth, close to the muck and the spittle, close to the mangy dogs and the deformed indigents in the street outside. Delhi is scarcely an innocent city, for on every layer it is riddled with graft and intrigue, but it is distinctly organic, to an atavistic degree. An apposite introduction to the city, I think, is provided by Map Eight of the *Delhi City Atlas*, which marks a substantial slab of the municipal area as being Dense Jungle: though this is now a city of a million inhabitants, it feels near the bush still. From many parts of it the open plain is in sight, and the country trees of India, the feathery tamarisks and ubiquitous acacias, invade every part of it – the animals too, for squirrels are everywhere and monkeys, buffalos, cows, goats and a million pye-dogs roam the city streets peremptorily.

There is simplicity everywhere, too, for rural people from all India flock into Delhi for jobs, for help, to see the sights. There are Sikhs and sleek Bengalis, Rajputs ablaze with jewellery, smart Gujaratis from the western coast, beautiful Tamils from the south, cloaked Tibetans smelling of untanned leather, clerks from Bombay smelling of aftershave, students, wandering sages,

35

clumping soldiers in ammunition boots, black-veiled Moslem women, peasants in for the day from the scorched and desiccated Punjab plains. Endearingly they trail through their national monuments, awe-struck, and the attendants intone their mono-logues hoping for tips, and the tourist buses line up outside the Presidential Palace, and the magicians prepare their levitations and inexplicable disappearances in the dusty ditch below the ramparts of the Red Fort.

This is the Gandhian truth of India, expressed in Delhi chiefly by such reminders of an earthier world beyond the city limits. Though I fear I might not give up my electric typewriter without a struggle, still I am a Gandhian myself in principle, and respond easily to this suggestion of a vast Indian *naïveté*, stretching away from Delhi like a limitless reservoir, muddied perhaps but deeply wholesome. The Gandhian ethic is rather outmoded in India, in fact, and the Mahatma himself seems to be losing his charismatic appeal, but still I liked the inscriptions in the visitors' book at Birla House, where he died in 1948 (his body was displayed to the public on the roof, illuminated by search-light), and where many a country pilgrim reverently pauses. 'My heart heaving with emotion,' wrote P. H. Kalaskar. 'Moving indeed,' thought A. K. Barat. Several people wrote 'Felt happy.' One said 'Most worth seeing place in Delhi,' and when, quoting from the master himself, I contributed 'Truth is God,' the inevitable onlookers murmured, 'Very good, very good,' nodded approvingly to each other and touched my hand in sympathy.

Delhi is a city of basic, spontaneous emotions: greed, hate, revenge, love, pity, kindness, the murderous shot, the touch of the hand. Its very subtleties are crude: even its poverty is black and white. On the one side are the organized beggar children who, taught to murmur a few evocative words of despair like 'hungry', 'baby' or 'mummy', succeed all too often in snaring the susceptible stranger. On the other are the courtly thousands of the jagghis, the shantytowns of matting, tentage and old packing cases which cling like black growths to the presence of Delhi.

There are beggars in Delhi who are comfortably off, and people too proud to beg who possess nothing at all, not a pot or a pan, not a pair of shoes. I saw one such man, almost naked, shivering with the morning cold and obviously very ill, huddled against a lamppost in Janpath early one morning. He asked for nothing, but I felt so sorry for him, and for a moment so loved him for his suffering, that I gave him a ten-rupee note, an inconceivable amount by the standards of Indian indigence. He looked at it first in disbelief, then in ecstasy and then in a wild gratitude, and I left him throwing his hands to heaven, singing, praying and crying, still clinging to his lamppost, and sending me away, slightly weeping myself, to coffee, toast and orange juice ('You'll be sure it's chilled, won't you?') at my hotel.

The voice of the people, Gandhi used to say, is the voice of God. I doubt it, but I do recognize a divine element to the Indian poverty, ennobled as it is by age and sacrifice. Indians rationalize it by the concept of reincarnation, and I see it too as a half-way condition, a station of the cross. 'In the next world,' I suggested to my driver after a long and exhausting journey into the country, 'I'll be driving and you'll be lying on the back seat,' but he answered me with a more elemental philosophy. 'In the next world,' he replied, 'we'll *both* be lying on the back seat!' For even the inegality of Delhi, even the pathos, often has something robust to it, a patient fatalism that infuriates many modernists but is a solace to people like me. It is disguised often in Eastern mumbo-jumbo, preached about in ashrams to gullible Californians and exploited by swamis from the divine to the absurd: but 37 it is really no more than a kindly acceptance of things as they are, supported by the sensible thesis that things are not always what they appear to be.

But pathos, yes. Delhi is the capital of the losing streak. It is the metropolis of the crossed wire, the missed appointment, the puncture, the wrong number. Every day's paper in Delhi brings news of some new failure, in diplomacy, in economics, in sport: when India's women entered the world table-tennis tournament during my stay in Delhi, not only were they all beaten but one actually failed to turn up for the match. I was pursued in the city by a persistent and not unattractive Rajput businessman. I thought him rather suave as I fended him off, in his well-cut check suit and his trendy ties, confident of manner, worldly of discourse: but one day I caught sight of him *hors de combat*, so to speak, muffled in a threadbare overcoat and riding a battered motor scooter back to his suburban home – and suddenly saw him, far more endearingly if he did but know it, as he really was, smallish, poorish, struggling and true.

He dropped me in the end anyway, perhaps because I developed an unsightly boil in my nose – men seldom send roses to girls with red noses. The side of my face swelled up like a huge bunion, and I was half red and half white, and sniffly and sad and sorry for myself. In this condition, self-consciously, I continued my investigations, and at first I was touched by the tact with which Indians in the streets pretended not to notice. After a day or two, though, I realized that the truth was more affecting still. They *really* did not notice. They thought my face quite normal. For what is a passing grotesquerie, in a land of deformities?

'Certainly,' said the government spokesman, perusing my list of questions, 'by all means, these are all very simple matters. We can attend to them for you at once. As I told you, it is our duty! It is what we are paid for! I myself have to attend an important meeting this afternoon – you will excuse me, I hope? – but I will leave all these little matters with our good Mrs Gupta and all will be taken care of. I will telephone you with the answers myself without fail – or if not I myself, then Mrs Gupta will be sure to telephone you either today or tomorrow morning. Did you sign our register? A duplicate signature here if you would not mind, and the lady at the door will issue you with the requisite application form for a pass – it will make everything easier for you, you see. Have no fear, Mrs Gupta will take care of everything. But mark my words, you will find the spiritual aspects of our city the most rewarding. Remember the River Ganges! As a student of history, you will find that I am right! Ha ha! Another cup of tea? You have time?'

Even he would agree, though, that the spiritual aspect is hardly predominant in New Delhi, the headquarters of the Indian government and the seat of Indian sovereignty – the newest and largest of Delhi's successive capitals. This was built by the British, and despite one or two sententious symbolisms and nauseating texts – 'Liberty Will Not Descend to a People, A People Must Raise Themselves to Liberty' – it is a frank and indeed noble memorial to their own imperial Raj. It is not anomalous even now. For one thing it was built in a hybrid style of East and West, to take care of all historical contingencies, and for another, Britishness is far from dead in Delhi. Delhi gentlemen, especially of the sporting classes, are stupendously British still. Delhi social events can be infinitely more English than Ascot or Lords. The following scrambled-names puzzle appeared recently in a Delhi magazine: LIWL EFFEY (a comedian);

UALNIJ YHLXEU (a zoologist); ARMY SHES (a pianist); HIIPPLL LLEGAADU (a historian). Only two classes of people on earth could solve this riddle without reference books: Britons of a certain age, Indians of a certain class.

Besides, the grand ensemble of New Delhi, the Presidential Palace flanked by the two wings of the Secretariat, has adapted easily to the republican style. It was the greatest single artefact of the British Empire, perhaps its principal work of art, and there are men still alive in Delhi who spent all their working lives building it. I met one, a rich and venerable Sikh contractor, and he recalled the great work with immense pride, and spoke affectionately of its English architects, and said it never once occurred to him to suppose, during all the years he worked upon it, that an Indian would ever be sitting in the halls of the Viceroy's Lodge.

Seen early on a misty morning from far down the ceremonial mall, Rajpath, New Delhi is undeniably majestic – neither Roman, its architects said, nor British, nor Indian, but *imperial*. Then its self-consciousness (for its mixture of styles is very contrived) is blurred by haze and distance and by the stir of awakening Delhi – the civil servants with their bulging briefcases, the multitudinous peons, the pompous early-morning policemen, the women sweepers elegant in primary colours, the minister perhaps (if it is not *too* early) in his chauffeur-driven, Indian-built limousine, the stocky Gurkha sentries at the palace gates, the first eager tourists from the Oberoi Intercontinental, the entertainer with his dancing monkeys, the snake charmer with his acolyte children, the public barber on the pavement outside Parliament, the women preparing their washing beside the ornamental pools, the man in khaki who, approaching you fiercely across the formal gardens, asks if you would care for a cold drink.

Then the power of India, looming above these dusty complexities, is unmistakable: not only created but instinctive, sensed by its foreign rulers as by its indigenous, and aloof to history's permutations. Of all the world's countries, India is the most truly prodigious, and this quality of astonishment displays itself afresh every day as the sun comes up in Delhi. Five hundred and eighty million people, three hundred languages, provinces from the Himalayan to the equatorial, cities as vast as Bombay and Calcutta, villages so lost in time that no map marks them, nuclear scientists and aboriginal hillmen, industrialists of incalculable wealth and dying beggars sprawled on railway platforms, three or four great cultures, myriad religions, pilgrims from across the world, politicians sunk in graft, the Grand Trunk Road marching to Peshawar, the temples of Madras gleaming in the sun, an inexhaustible history, an incomprehensible social system, an unfathomable repository of human resource, misery, ambiguity, vitality and confusion – all this, the colossal corpus of India, invests, sprawls around, infuses, elevates, inspires and very nearly overwhelms New Delhi.

Searching for a corrective to such cosmic visions, I thought I would investigate the roots or guts of New Delhi, instead of contemplating its tremendous aura, so I inveigled my way not into the State Hallroom or the Durbar Hall but into the kitchens of the Presidential Palace, by way of an obliging aide-de-camp and a compliant housekeeper (for as dubious flunkies repeatedly murmured as I made my way downstairs, 'It is not allowed to visitors'). At first I thought I had succeeded in finding humanity among that majesty, for the way to the kitchens passed through a labyrinth of homely offices, workshops and storerooms and cupboards, supervised by smiling and apparently contented domestics. Here were the Pot Cleaners, scouring their big copper pans. Here were the Linen Keepers, standing guard on their pillowslips. Here were the Washing Up Men, ankle deep in suds themselves, and here the Bakers invited me to taste the morning's loaf. I felt I was passing through some living exhibition of Indian Crafts, diligent, chaste and obliging.

But even before I entered the kitchen proper, a clanking and grand aroma brought me back to the realities of New Delhi, for in the palace of Rashtrapati Bhavan, Downstairs is scarcely less consequential than Up. These kitchens are imperial institutions themselves, half Western, half Eastern, colossal in scale, lordly in pretension. Armies of cooks seemed to be labouring there. Foods of a dozen cuisines seemed to be in preparation. Batteries of aged electric ovens hummed and whirred. There were squadrons of deep freezers and battalions of chopping boards and armouries of steel choppers. The cooks and their underlings bowed to me as I passed, but not obsequiously. It was with condescension that they greeted me, one by one along the preparation tables, and when at last I reached the sizzling centre of that underworld, I felt myself to be more truly at a crossroad of the empires than anywhere else in Delhi – for there, just around the corner from the English ovens of the viceroys, they were smoking over charcoal braziers, scented with wheat grain, the aromatic yellow pomfrets that were a grand delicacy of the Moghuls.

So even in the kitchens power presides, in a traditional, ample sense. Delhi is full of it, for this republic, which came to office in a loincloth, rules in a gaudier uniform. Nehru said that modern Western civilization was ersatz, living by ersatz values, eating ersatz food: but the ruling classes of Delhi, the politicians, the businessmen, the military, have mostly adopted those values without shame. Gandhi said that his India would have 'the smallest possible army', but Delhi is one of the most military of all capitals: when I looked up some friends in the Delhi telephone book, I found that under the name Khanna there were four generals, an air commodore, twelve colonels, a group captain, twelve majors, three wing commanders, four captains, one commander, three lieutenant commanders and a lieutenant.

Nor is Delhi's display just a façade or a bluff. India often seems to outsiders a crippled country, emaciated by poverty and emasculated by philosophy, but it is only a half-truth. We are told that half India's population is undernourished and three quarters illiterate: that leaves nearly 180 million people who are well fed and literate. The Indian gross national product is the tenth largest on earth. The armies of India are very strong and are largely equipped from Indian factories. I went one day to the Delhi Industrial Fair, housed in a series of modernist ziggurats directly across the street from the gateway of the ruined city Purana Qila, and there I discovered that India makes not only warships, railway engines and aircraft, but Carbicle Grinders too, Lapping Machines and Micro-Fog Lubricators ('I'll take that one,' said I flippantly, pointing to an electric transformer as big as a cottage, 'please send it to my hotel' – and diligently the salesman took out his order form).

Power corrupts, of course, and in India it corrupts on a grand scale. At the top, the whisper of nepotism or opportunism repeatedly approaches Central Government itself. At the bottom, graft harasses the street hawkers of the city, who can scarcely afford the protection money demanded by the police. Even the stranger to Delhi feels the rot: in the arrogant petty official declining to look up from his newspaper, in the stifling addiction to red tape and precedent, in the affectations and snobberies which, as they thrive in Washington's Georgetown, flourish here too in the districts south of Rajpath.

As it happens, I am rather an addict of power. I do not much enjoy submitting to it or even exerting it, but I do like observing it. I like the aesthetics of it, coloured as they so often are by pageantry and history. I am everybody's patriot, and love to see the flags flying over palace or parliament, Westminster or Quai d'Orsay. I am very ready to be moved by the emanations of power in Delhi – the sun setting behind the Red Fort, the grand mass of New Delhi seen across the dun plateau or the ceremony of Beating Retreat on Vijay Chowk, when a dozen military bands pluck at the heart with the Last Post and 'Abide with Me'.

Nobody cries more easily than I do, when the bugle sounds or the flag comes down, but somehow I do not respond to the old magic in India. The British, rationalizing their own love of imperial pomp, used to claim that it was necessary to retain the respect of Asiatics. It availed them nothing, though, against the 'half-naked fakir', as Churchill called Gandhi, and now too the magnificence of Delhi seems paradoxically *detached* from India. How remote the great ensigns which, enormously billowing above their embassies in the diplomatic enclave, testify to the presence of the plenipotentiaries! How irrelevant the posturings of the grandees, hosts and guests alike, the Polish defence minister greeted by epauletted generals, the Prince of Wales inevitably winning his polo match, the resident Congress party spokesman puffed up at one press conference, the visiting minister of national reorientation condescending at the next.

And most detached of all seems the unimaginable bureaucracy of Delhi, battening upon the capital – a power sucker, feeding upon its own consequence or sustained intravenously by inter-departmental memoranda, triplicate applications, copies and comments and addenda and references to precedent – a monstrous behemoth of authority, slumped immovable among its files and tea-trays. Much of it is concerned not with practical reality at all but with hypotheses or dogma. Forty government editors are engaged in producing the collected works of Gandhi, down to the last *pensée* – they have got to volume fifty-four. Hundreds more are concerned with plans, for there was never a capital like Delhi for planners – the Multilevel Planning Section, the Plan Coordination Division, the Plan Information Unit, the Social Planning Unit, the Project Appraisal Unit, the Socio-Economic Research Unit, the Programme Evaluation Organization, the National Sample Survey Organization, the National Survey Organization, the Central Statistical Organization. Big Brother is everywhere, with a slide rule, a clipboard and a warning in small print. 'This map', says one Delhi tourist publication severely, 'is published for tourists as a master guide and *not as legal tender*' – and there, in its mixture of the interfering, the pedantic, the unnecessary and the absurd, speaks the true voice of Indian officialdom.

But this is an essential part of the Indian mystery, always has been, probably always will be. Delhi is too old to care anyway, and takes the system as it comes. Which viceroy or president had he most enjoyed serving, I asked one antediluvian retainer at Rashtrapati Bhavan. He shrugged his shoulders with an almost perceptible creak. 'I serve the government,' he said. 'It is all the same to me.' With this indifference in mind I went that afternoon to a murder trial which, to much publicity, was proceeding then in the New District Court, a kind of permanent bad dream in concrete in the northern part of the city – filthy, cramped, dark and suffocatingly overcrowded. Here authority was at its most immediate and most awful. The case concerned the alleged murder of a well-known south-of-Rajpath lady by her husband, a fashionable eye surgeon, assisted by his mistress and an assortment of vagabond accomplices. It was a true *crime passionel* with thuggish overtones, and at least five people faced, there and then, the ultimate penalty. The judge was a grave and clever Sikh, turbaned and spectacled. The court was jammed with a festering, jostling audience, hungry for the salacious, the macabre and the terrible. The white-tabbed attorneys droned and argued, the watchmen barred the door with staves, the accused sat in chains along the side of the court, shackled to their guards.

Yet fearful though their predicament was, they did not seem awe-struck nor even alarmed. They were like sightseers themselves, of their own tragedy. They yawned occasionally. They exchanged comments. They laughed at the legal jokes. And sometimes, feeling the strain of the long day, they raised their manacled wrists to their warders' shoulders and, placing their cheeks upon their hands like sleepy children, dozed through destiny for a while.

'I will find that out for you, of course,' said the government spokesman. 'It will be no problem at all. You see, it is something I am not exactly sure of myself, but we have many sources of information. Do we have your telephone number? Ah yes. I have temporarily mislaid it. Would you give it to me again? Rest assured, dear lady, I shall find out this information, together with the answers to your earlier questions, and shall telephone you for certain, if not this afternoon, then tomorrow morning first thing.

'I don't know if you are familiar, you see, with the *Bhagavad-Gita*? As a student of the Gandhian philosophy you would find it very beautiful: and you would find it exceedingly relevant to your article about Delhi. It is self-awareness, you see, that is the key. Oh, madam, you are laughing at me! You are very wicked! But never mind, you will see, you will see! And in the meantime you may be quite sure,' he concluded with his usual charming smile and reassuring shake of the head, 'that I will be telephoning you with this information, or if not I myself, then our good Mrs Gupta is sure to. It is not very spiritual but we must do our duty!'

There is a species of telephone operators' English, often heard in Delhi, which is not exactly an articulated language at all, but a sort of elongated blur. Indian English proper, of course, is one of India's cruellest handicaps, for it is so often imperfect of nuance and makes for an unreal relationship between host and visitor, besides often making highly intelligent people look foolish ('CHINESE GENERALS FLY BACK TO FRONT', said a celebrated Indian headline long ago). But the elliptical, slithery kind is something else again, and has another effect on its hearers. It makes one feel oddly opaque or amorphous oneself, and seems to clothe the day's arrangements in a veil of uncertainty.

This is proper. One should not go fighting into Delhi, chin up and clear-eyed. Here hopes are meant to wither and conceptions adjust. A single brush with a noseless beggar is enough to change your social values. Just one application for an import licence will alter your standards of efficiency. After a while graver mutations may occur, and you will find yourself questioning the Meaning of It All, the Reality of Time and other old Indian specialties. 'You will see, you will see!' Most disconcerting of all, you may well come to feel that the pomp and circumstance of Delhi, which struck you at first as illusory display, is in fact the only reality of the place! All the rest is mirage. Everything else in the Indian presence, north, east, south, west, across the Rajasthani deserts, down to the Coromandel beaches, far away to the

47

frontiers of Tibet, everything else is suggestion, never to be substance.

I pick a Delhi newspaper at random. Crowd Loots Colliery. Police Kill Dacoits. Dacoits Loot Pilgrims. Students Raid Cinema. Farmers Arrested during Agitation. Teachers Boycott Examination. Police Fire on Crowd. Mizo Rebels Spotted. Peace Feelers for Naga Rebels. A State of Emergency exists in India, but one is hardly aware of it, for this is a country always in emergency, crossed perpetually by dim figures of faith and violence, prophets of revolution, priests of reaction, saints and spies and fanatics, moving here and there through a haze of hatred, idealism and despair. Experts Visit Bomb Blast Site. Police Charge Crowd. 600 Arrested. Government Minister Has Asthma.

Sometimes these shadows reach into Delhi itself, and chaos feels uncomfortably close. While I was there the hereditary Imam of the Jama Masjid, the greatest mosque in India, was engaged in a quarrel with the government. He was even heard inciting his congregation to political dissent over the loudspeakers of his minaret during a visit to the neighbourhood by Mrs Gandhi herself. His family have been incumbents of the Imamate since the mosque was founded by Shah Jehan in 1650, and are great figures in the Muslim community: nevertheless he was arrested, and in the ensuing riots at least six people were killed (always add a zero, an Indian acquaintance nonchalantly told me, if you want the true figure) and at least six hundred locked away for safety's sake.

It happened that I was wandering around the purlieus of the mosque on the day of the arrest, and bleak was the sensation of *déjà vu* with which I watched the riot police, brandishing their guns and batons, heavily clambering out of their trucks. But

48

more ominous still, I thought, was the spectacle of the mosque itself a few days later. They slapped a curfew on the area, and when I next passed its outskirts, along the crammed and filthy pavements of Netaji Subhash Marg, where the beggar families crouch day and night beneath their sacking shelters and the teeming junk bazaars crowd around the Chadni Chowk – when I looked across to the Jama Masjid, I saw its great shape there silent and eerily deserted – gone the milling figures of the faithful on its steps, gone the stir of commerce and devotion that habitually surrounds it, empty all the stalls and shops, the kebab restaurants, the fortune-tellers, the silversmiths, the tanners and the cobblers. All were empty, and the mosque looked like some immense captive champion, brooding there in solitary confinement.

Yet even this all-too-real reality seemed a deception upon the composure of Delhi. I never feel insecure there, even when the riot police are storming by. The only citizens who frighten me are those damned monkeys, so beguiling of motion, so threatening of grimace. Delhi people treat these beasts with distinct circumspection, crossing roads to avoid them or bribing them with peanuts to go away, and in this, it seemed to me, poor Indians behave towards monkeys much as Europeans behave towards poor Indians – especially as, the monkey god Hanuman being an important figure of the Hindu pantheon, some element of conscience is presumably involved. This disconcerting parallel gave me an unexpected sense of membership, and every time a monkey bared its teeth at me I felt like saying, 'Wait, friend, wait – I'm the European, it's the poor Indian you want!'

For the Indian sense of hierarchy, which so contributes to the bafflement of India, provides for each rank of society a kind of comradeship; and in Delhi especially, which is like a shadow   49 play of India, one senses the hidden force of it. The Untouchables of the capital – Harijans, Children of God, as Gandhi called them – live in well-defined colonies on the edge of the city. Though I knew better intellectually, emotionally I somehow expected, when I drove out there one afternoon, to find them a people made morose and hangdog by their status. In fact they turned out to be a very jolly lot, welcoming and wreathed in smiles, and looking at least as cheerful as the average member of the Socio-Economic Research Unit, say. Why not? They might be Harijans to the world outside, but they were doubtless Brahmins to each other.

In the same way Delhi, preoccupied with its own diurnal round of consequence and command, is paradoxically protected against that dust storm of controversy, threat and misfortune which hangs always, dark and ill-defined, over the Indian horizons. That blur or slither of Delhi, which begins as a mystery and develops into an irritation, becomes in the end a kind of reassurance. After trying three times, you give up gratefully. After expostulating once or twice, it is a pleasure to accede. You think you can change the system? Try it, try it, and when the elaborations of Delhi have caught up with you, when you realize the tortuous significances of the old method, when it has been explained to you that only Mrs Gupta is qualified to take the money, that Mr Mukerjee is prevented by custom from working beside Mr Mukhtar Singh and that Mr Mohammed will not of course be at work on Fridays, when it dawns upon you gradually that it has been done more or less this way, come conqueror, come liberation, since the early Middle Ages, with a relieved and affectionate smile you will probably agree that perhaps it had better be left as it is.

As it is! India is always as it is! I never despair in Delhi, for I feel always all around me the fortification of a profound apathy. The capital is essentially apathetic to the nation: the nation is aloof to the capital. By the end of the century there will be, at the present rate of increase, nearly 1,000 million people in India, and I think it very likely that there will have been a revolution of one complexion or another. But the traveller who returns to Delhi then will find the city much the same, I swear, will respond to much the same emotions, indulge in just the same conjectures, bog down in just the same philosophical quagmires, and reach, if he is anything like me, about the same affectionate and inconclusive conclusions.

'You see? You see? Did I not say so? You are thinking metaphysically, as I foretold!' Well, perhaps. But the government spokesman proved his point better himself, for neither he nor Mrs Gupta ever did ring.

Over the Bridge

SYDNEY, 1983

When I first wrote about Sydney, in 1958, I disliked the city so much that it was five full years before the last furious response reached me from Australia. By 1983, after half a dozen visits, I may have mellowed a bit, and the city certainly had: I was rather disappointed to find local reactions to this essay almost entirely friendly (but then this time I did not describe Sydney's society ladies, as I had in 1958, as looking 'steely, scornful and accusatory, as though they are expecting you — which Heaven forbid — to offer them an improper suggestion . . .').

'Kev. *Kev!* Time you got going.'

'Jeez, Sandra, it's raining out there.'

'TV says it's fining up. You're not crook are you, Kev? It's all that booze you know, Kev, you know what the doctor said, cut down on the booze he said, no wonder you're crook in the mornings, the human body can take only so much . . .' But Kev has slipped out by now, and with his office gear slung in his back-pack is away, and up the steps, and half-way along the approach to the great bridge.

If he was crook, he is crook no more, for the TV was right, the rain clears as if by magic, and all the glory of the winter morning unfolds over the water as he breaks into his jog along the sidewalk. He is joining the stream of life itself! To his right the suburban trains clatter, the commuter cars lurch in fits and starts towards the city. To his left ferries bustle across the harbour, the first hydrofoil is streaking in a foamy curve towards the sea, the very first yacht is slipping from its moorings, and a tug is on its way, riding lights still burning, to meet the towering freighter just appearing around the headland.

On the harbour bridge there are already plenty of people about. He overtakes briskly walking businessmen with brief-cases and identical moustaches. He is overtaken by huge athletes in sweat bands and sloganed shirts. Archetypal schoolboys loiter their way, satchels dangling, reluctantly towards their education. An elderly lady in a mackintosh cries 'Grand to see the sun again!' in an exaggeratedly Irish brogue. Another pack of giants comes panting and sweating past. Another covey of schoolboys kicks a pebble here and there. Ahead of him, between the massive pylons of the bridge, the city towers are beginning to gleam in the sun, and there is a flashing of upper windows, and a fluttering of flags in and out of shadow, and a golden shine from the observation deck of the tallest tower of all.

It is as though the innocence of the morning has infected the whole scene, and made everything young. A pristine vigour is on the air, very fresh and good for you, like orange juice. By the time Kev reaches his office on the seventeenth floor, he feels he's never drunk a tinny of Foster's in his life: and looking back upon the scurrying ferries of the Circular Quay, the flying white roofs of the Opera House, the traffic still streaming across the bridge, the rising sun and the water and the green parklands all around, silently he congratulates himself once more, as he does every morning as a matter of principle, upon his great good fortune in being born an Australian.

The city he surveys is a very concentrate of that condition. The whole matter of Australia, history, character, reputation, attitude, 53 finds its best epitome in this particular corner of the great land mass, where Sydney stands beside its fjord-like harbour. When the world thinks of Australia, it thinks of that bridge, that Opera House, that wake-frothed and yacht-flecked harbour. When the world thinks of an Australian, it thinks, more or less, of Kev.

Australian society is overwhelmingly urban, and Sydney is Australia *urbanissima*. Canberra is the capital, Adelaide is a delight, Perth holds the America's Cup, Melbourne people believe their city to be at least as mature, civilized and unutterably lovely, but only Sydney has the true metropolitan presence. An enormous spread of surburbia around an intensely packed downtown, it stands upon its marvellous haven in the stance of proper consequence. A glittering business quarter makes one feel it is keyed in to the Wall Street–London–Zurich–Hong Kong circuit of profit. The inescapable presence of virtually the whole Australian Navy, moored beside its dockyards or glamorously returning from sea with ensigns flying and radars twirling, gives it a front-line air. It is equipped with all the statutory metropolitan tokens – city marathon, revolving restaurant, supine veiled figure by Henry Moore, breakfast TV and Bahai temple.

Its stature really resides, though, not in its universality, not in its membership in the league of big cities, but for better or worse, like it or not, in its unchallengeable Australianness. It is a metropolis *sui generis*. Take its looks for a start. Architecturally Sydney is no great shakes. Its suburbs are at best pleasantly ordinary, enlivened only, here and there, by wrought iron and engaging terracing. Its downtown is handsome but unexceptional, the usual cubes, cylinders, plazas and mirror-walls of contemporary urbanism surrounding the usual clumps of nineteenth-century florid. It has no elegant set pieces of civic planning, and has crudely degraded its waterfront on Sydney Cove, the site of its beginnings and still the focus of its life, by building an express-way slap across it.

Yet it is one of the most beautiful cities in the world, specifically because it is Australian. That winding, nooky, islanded, bosky harbour thrillingly reminds one always that Sydney stands on the shore of an island totally unlike anywhere else on earth. The pale pure light of the Sydney winter seems to come straight from the bergs and ice mountains of Antarctica. The foliage of Sydney's parks and gardens is queerly drooped and tangled, apparently antediluvian fig trees overshadow suburban streets, and the perpetual passing of the ships through the very heart of the city gives everything a tingling sense of remoteness. The water goes down the plug-hole the other way in Australia, and it really is possible to imagine, if you are a fancifully minded visitor from the other hemisphere, that this metropolis is clinging upside-down to the bottom of the earth, so subtly antipodean, or perhaps marsupial, is the nature of the scene.

The supreme Sydney experience, for such a traveller, is a walk on a brisk sunny morning around the headland called Mrs Macquarie's Chair, through a complex of park and garden beside the harbour. Except only for Stanley Park in Vancouver, this seems to me the loveliest of all city parklands, but its loveliness is of a sly, deceptive kind. It is like a park in the mind. The grass is almost too vividly green, the trees look curiously artificial, parakeets squawk viciously at each other in the shrubbery. The shifting scene around you, as you walk the park's perimeter, seems more ideal than actual – water everywhere, and those grey warships at their quays, and glimpses of Riviera-like settlements all around, and a sham castle in a garden, and the inescapable passing of the ferries.

And slyest of all is the prospect as you round the point itself, 55 where the families are spreading their picnics on the grass, and a solitary ibis is burrowing for edibles in a rubbish can; for there suddenly like an aery fantasy the Sydney Opera House, most peculiar of architectural masterpieces, spreads its white wings in the sunshine, light as some unsuspected water-bird, with the massive old harbour bridge, a beast to its insubstantial beauty, all brutal heft above.

Those two unforgettable structures, the one rooted so powerfully in the bed-rock, the other aspiring to the state of levitation, represent the nature of this city more than aesthetically. Upon Sydney's foundation of absolute British Australianness has been superimposed a prismatically ethnic superstructure, making this city, formerly one of the most homogeneous and stodgy in the world, a fascinating mix of the complacent and the tentative, the almost immovable and the practically irresistible.

Once it used to suggest nowhere else. Now it is full of alien allusion. It reminds me often of Stockholm. As Sydney is to the south, Stockholm is to the north, and Sydney's Australia is Stockholm's Scandinavia – I am not surprised that the Danish architect of the Opera House clearly had in his memory, as he planned his prodigy, Stockholm's Town Hall upon an inlet of another sea. The light of this southern fjord is not unlike the light of the Baltic; a pallid freshness is common to both cities; sitting snugly out of the sunlight in Sydney's Strand Arcade, all fancy balustrades and tesselated paving, sometimes I almost expect to see the shoppers shaking the snow from their galoshes, breathing in their hands to restore the circulation, and ordering themselves a schnapps.

At other moments Sydney reminds me of somewhere in
Central Europe: any Saturday morning in the plush waterside

suburb called Double Bay, for example, when the rich immigrants assemble in the street café of the Cosmopolitan, talking loudly in Ruritanian, or deep in the financial pages of the *Sydney Morning Herald*. Like the bourgeoisie of old Prague or Budapest they while the hours away in chat and exhibitionism – here four men with coats slung over their shoulders, smoking small cigars and passionately arguing about President Benes – here a couple of leathery ladies, furred and proudly diamonded, sitting in lofty silence over aperitifs – a young poseur in a deerstalker hat, smoking a cigarette in a long jade holder, a gaggle of Double Bay socialites in the swathed ragbag fashion, faintly Martial Arts in suggestion, rampant in Sydney at the moment.

Lebanese proliferate in Sydney, and Greeks, and Philipinos, and Indonesians. The Vietnamese, they tell me, are shifting out of the western suburbs towards East Sydney. Maori gays, gossip picturesquely maintains, are taking over Bondi. The Spanish Club advertises itself with a picture of Don Quixote and Sancho riding out of a golden Outback. Sydney's Chinatown booms with investment from Hong Kong, and the Chinese taste for unexpectedly mixed foods seems to have infected the entire municipal cuisine, so that perfectly true–blue Aussie restaurants are likely to offer you hot buttered pumpkin and orange soup with peppercorns floating in it, or quail in a sauce made of red wine and bacon. The Sydney Municipal Board sometimes likes to announce itself in all the languages of its tax-paying citizenry – 'MESTSKÁ RADA SYDNEY' or 'SYDNEY VÁVOSI TANÁCS' – and these arcane proclamations, attached to some lumpish municipal pile of mid-Victorian imperialism, pungently illustrate the state of things.

Still dominant nevertheless, as the bridge looms high over the Opera House, stand the likes of Kev. The flow of immigration has softened, eased and illuminated Sydney, but it came too late ever to displace the original blood-stream of this city. Half a century ago 98 per cent of Sydney people were of British descent, and it is they, the Old Australians, who still set the anthropological tone. Sit long enough among the Ruritanians at the Cosmopolitan, and some beefy young Ocker will arrive to steal the scene and drink his beer out of the bottle. Go to *La Traviata* at the Opera House, and my, what an unexpectedly hearty and robust chorus of ladies and gentlemen will be attendant upon Violetta in the opening act, their crinolines and Parisian whiskers delightfully failing to disguise physiques born out of Australian surf and sunshine, and names like Higginson and O'Rourke – while even La Traviata herself, as she subsides to the last curtain, may seem to you the victim of some specifically Australian variety of tuberculosis, since she looks as though immediately after the curtain-call she will be off for a vigorous set of tennis with the conductor, or at least a grilled lobster with orange sauce and caramel.

Such is the strength of Kev's sub-species, into which the children of all those immigrants, too, are inexorably mutated. Years ago, waiting for the Manly ferry, I caught the eye of a young Italian working at a coffee-stall, and I remember distinctly the wiry black Latinate quality of his person. I went down there again the other day to see if he was still about, and found him not just aged and plumped, but altogether altered by the Kev Effect – his face pulled into a different shape, his sparkle replaced by something more wary or blunted, or perhaps dreamier. And when he spoke, the last traces of Neapolitanism were all but hidden beneath the virile twisted vowels of Australian English.

Language, they say, is the badge of nationality, and above all else it is the language of Sydney that binds this fissile society into a recondite unity. It is many years since the writer Monica Dickens, at a Sydney signing session, inscribed a volume to Emma Chissett, misunderstanding a lady who wanted to know the price of the book, but fundamentally the vernacular has not changed: 'Emma Chissett?' I make a point of asking now, when I want to buy something, and the shop assistants never give me a second glance, taking my dinkum Aussiness for granted, and frequently confiding in me their grievances about the train service from Parramatta.

Or from Woop Woop perhaps, an imaginary township which has become a Sydney generic for the back of beyond. Sydney English is full of such fantasies and in-jokes, and consciously perpetuates itself in self-amusement, hardly a year passing without another new dictionary of the argot. Usages change constantly – out goes *she'll be apples* ('it'll be OK'), in comes *throwing a mental* (losing one's temper) – and there is almost nobody in Sydney, schoolboy to sage, who is not eager to discuss the present state of the vernacular. Why do Sydney women end all their sentences, even the most definite, with a rising interrogative inflexion? Because they're so put down they daren't say anything for sure. What's the true definition of an Ocker? 'A man who watches the footy on TV with a terry-towel hat on his head and a tinny of Foster's balanced on his belly.'

The language makes the man, and makes the city too. Without his language your Sydney citizen (he no longer calls himself a Sydneysider) might be taken for a Scandinavian, a Californian or even sometimes an Englishman: with it even a second-generation immigrant can be mistaken for nobody else, and the fizz and the fun of the tongue reflects Sydney's particular strain of constancy. The pubs of this city are loud with jazz and rock music, 59 deafening the packed saloons within, blaring over the sidewalks. Often the thump of it drives the customers into a frenzy, and the bars are full of strapping young Ockers throwing their hands above their heads, whoopeeing and beating their enormous feet. They are not at all like roisterers of Europe or America, partly because they all seem to be, like that opera chorus, in a condition of exuberant physical well-being, partly because the tang of their language pervades everything they do, and for a time I thought their burly disco to be something altogether new out of Sydney, an Australization specifically of the 1980s.

But emerging half-shattered one day from the Observer Inn, having weaved a perilous way among those flailing limbs and stomping size 14s, I chanced to see, in a shop down the road, a print of early Sydney settlers living it up 150 years ago. They wore floppy slouch hats and check shirts, were heavily bearded, and were probably celebrating their recent release from hard labour in the prisons: but they were kicking their legs about in that self-same Sydney fandango, in just the same heavyweight high jinks, and were yelling their songs and cheerful obscenities, I am sure, in similarly rank and entertaining distortions.

For even Sydney has a past. It began in the 1780s with the arrival of the first British convicts, put ashore here in their chains to serve as the reluctant and incongruous Founding Fathers of Australia. It ended in the 1950s with the mass landings of the European immigrants, disembarking after their government-subsidized passages to transform Australia from semi-emancipated colonialism into Pacific cosmopolitanism. By then the penal colony had developed into a city of great but somewhat unlively character, chauvinist to an almost comical degree, with an elite of often snobby and vulgar monarchists, and a labour force so powerful that unionists everywhere called this the Worker's Paradise. In those days any Sydney matron worth her social salt boasted of her distant connection with the Earl of Mudcastle while the Sydney proletariat was as rough, as ready, as truculent, as contemptuous of Earls and as militantly Irish as a self-respecting proletariat ought to be.

Today that society has mostly gone underground. If you want a symbolic demonstration of it, try going to the subterranean railway station beside the Town Hall: for there behind the trendily creeper-covered walls of the sunken plaza, all waterfalls and canopies, the station itself survives as a very museum of the Old Australia – brass knobs, bakelite switches, Instructions to Employees in copperplate script behind brass-framed glass, bare electric bulbs lighting up to announce the next train to Pymble or Hornby. The Sydney railways are very Old Australia. So are the ferries, and the pubs, and the memorials to kings and queens and Robbie Burns. The granddaughters of those well-connected matrons still curtsey with a preposterous zeal when Prince Charles drops by. Go-slows on the Woop Woop line, heavy-jowled men with placards demanding a Fair Go For Aussie Ships, recall the heyday of the Worker's Paradise. The old beery machismo has not been entirely subsumed in white wine and unisex hairdressing.

More importantly, out of the Old Australia comes Sydney's sense of order and fair play, which underpins the shifting vigour of this city. 'KINDNESS AND COURTESY' is still the motto of Double Bay School, and to a remarkable degree the old values obtain. You might expect this haven on a creek at the bottom of the world to be a seamy, wild and reckless place, and of course Australians, like city people everywhere on earth, talk with dismay of rising crime rates and drunken driving. By most 61 standards, though, Sydney is good as gold. The streets are much safer than most, the traffic is generally demure enough, even jay-walkers look guilty, and the city comports itself, at least to visitors, with unfailing *politesse*.

These are legacies based, *au fond*, upon Parliamentary democracy and the Common Law, and their survival is a tribute to their strength: for what has happened all around them, in the last three decades, is nothing less than a social revolution. Sydney has become a different city, different in style, in aspiration, in loyalty, in taste. A generation ago, it seemed to me, the very core of the Sydney ethos was the memory of the sacrifices its men had made in the two world wars, fighting in a cause almost quixotically remote to them, yet made poignantly real by their devotion to Crown, Flag and Empire. The heroic ordeals of Gallipoli and Alamein stood somewhere near the root of the civic pride, and the Returned Servicemen's League was sacrosanct and inescapable.

But on a recent winter Sunday I revisited the great war memorial in Hyde Park which was the shrine of those epic memories, and found its tragic magnetism dispersed. It stood there still of course, grey, powerful and sombre among the trees; the sad sculpted soldiers still looked down, sitting like thoughtful gods around the parapet; but the people in the park somehow seemed to shy away from its presence, as though it had been put out of their minds by some process of re-education, or sealed up, with all its toxic energies, like an expended reactor.

It seems only proper that the motto of another Sydney school, 'I Hear, I See, I Learn', should translate into Latin as *Audio, Video, Disco*, for the young have boisterously discarded the old image of Sydney, and have remoulded it again in their own.

Today this city is one of the world's great promises, a pledge of better things, living in a state of ill-defined but perpetual expectancy.

It is a very young city: not just young in manners and accomplishment, but exceedingly young in person. Sometimes indeed it seems to be inhabited chiefly by schoolchildren, children kicking pebbles across bridges, children racing fig-leaves down the channels of ornamental fountains, children clambering like invading armies all over the Opera House, or mustered in their thousands in the New South Wales Art Gallery. They seem to me a stalwart crew. 'Now this is a Picasso,' I heard a teacher say in the gallery one day, 'I'm sure you all know who Picasso was.' 'I don't,' piped up a solitary small Australian at the back, and I bowed to him as the only absolutely honest soul in sight.

It is a city attuned to young ideas – 'Barefoot shoppers', sensibly decrees one of the grandest department stores, 'must not use the escalators' – and its youthfulness is so pervasive as to be almost hallucinatory. The magistrate in the petty sessions court looks like a second-year law student, the prosecuting attorney might just have invested in his first motor bike, and surely the accused, who is charged with public indecency, has not yet reached the age of puberty? As for the Stock Exchange, it appears to be run by several hundred athletes, helped by a few go-go girls in miniskirts, and the old men in the public gallery upstairs, ostensibly examining the shares board through their binoculars to see how Consolidated Metals are doing, look to me less like speculators than plain voyeurs.

The youthfulness of Sydney, like all youthfulness, is a little schizo, being half brash, but half timid. In a posh Sydney hotel, for instance, or an upstage Sydney restaurant, customers tend to behave with a detectable sense of reverence, talking in undertones to each other and gratefully accepting the wine-waiter's recommendation – it would be a *maître d*'s delight, were it not for the fact that in Sydney even that insufferable guild behaves with a becoming inhibition. Australians always used to be accused of inferiority complex, and though their image in the world is very different now, still Sydney has not reached the free fine assurance of absolute civic maturity – 'When I go to California', a very attractive and intelligent Sydney girl said to me, 'I feel like a mouse.'

And the mouse instinct erupts sometimes, of course, as it always does, into absurd expressions of self-assertion. Sydney people are far less vulnerable to criticism than they used to be – this used to be one of the prickliest of all the world's cities – but they are hardly less sensitive to the patronizing or the aloof. In Europe, one Sydney intellectual told me severely, ignorance about Australian affairs was abysmal, *abysmal* – why in London, he had been assured, reputable art critics had never even heard of Brett Whiteley!

'Brett Who?' I could not resist inquiring (remembering the boy in the art gallery) for this aspect of the Sydney style can be a bit relentless. One is told a little too often of the Whiteley genius, one tires of the gossip about the Sidney Whites and the Patrick Nolans; yes, one did realize that the author of *Schindler's Ark* was a local man; for myself I feel lucky to have missed the recent Sydney fashion show, about which I heard so much, which featured a ballet performance to aboriginal music, songs with flute accompaniment against a background of wrecked cars, and some extreme examples of the Bundled Jap look.

But then youth, hope and silliness go together, in cities as in people, and it is the hope that counts. The hope is what Kev unconsciously feels, as he jogs over the bridge in the morning, and what nearly every stranger feels too, on a first foray into the streets of Sydney. How young and strong the city! How magnificent the promise! One forgets sometimes that even in the Land of Oz, youth is not eternal.

The Reeperbahn or 42nd Street of Sydney is King's Cross, a mile or two south-east of Sydney Cove. This used to be an entertaining Bohemian quarter, but has degenerated lately into a nasty combination of squalor and pathos. Among the usual Reeperbahn company of pimps, pornographers, strippers, tattooists and transvestites, bathed in the conventionally sinful half-light, gaped at by the inevitable visitors from Woop Woop, through King's Cross after midnight there now move some more heart-rending figures: child-prostitutes, hardly in their teens, desperately made up and not very expertly soliciting the passing drunks and lechers.

John Gunther the great reporter used to ask, wherever he went in the world, 'Who runs this place?' It is my practice to ask who (or in print, perhaps, *whom*) I ought to be sorry for. In some cities – think of Calcutta, think of Johannesburg! – the question is superfluous. In many another the tender heart is wrung by terrible poverty, or political oppression, or general gloom of environment. In Sydney there is hardly any abject poverty. Politically the people of this city are free as air, socially they are as emancipated as anyone on earth. Their town is clean and mostly safe, their climate is a dream, and though they grumble a good deal about the effects of recession, and frequently go on strike, by the standards of the world at large they live magnificently.

So who should I be sorry for? Sydney people are puzzled by the question, and sometimes can't think of anyone at all.

Sometimes they reply with jokes about unsuccessful football players or politicians in eclipse. 'Me,' says Kev, but he does not mean it. A few propose those poor children of King's Cross, there are vague references sometimes to derelicts ('derros') or exploited immigrants. And in the end it occurs to most people that I should give a thought to the Abos, the Aborigines, whose names are all around one in Sydney, in Woolloomooloo, in Parramatta or in Woop Woop, but whose physical presence is but a wisp or a shadow in the thriving city.

Most of the Aborigines of these parts were exterminated, by imported disease or by brute force, within a few decades of the first white settlement. Yet two centuries later a few hundred cling to their roots in Sydney, at the very site of the European coming. They are called 'coories' here, and like the water of the harbour, like the exotic foliage of the parks and headlands, they are a reminder of stranger, older things than Kev and his kind can conceive. To some Australians the Aborigines are a blot on the conscience, to others just a pain in the neck: still, in the end most people thought the coories were worth feeling sorry for, and feel sorry for them I did.

Though their community has produced some celebrities in its time, notably boxers, they live mostly in more luckless quarters of the town, and do not show much as a rule. As it chanced however, while I was in Sydney this time they celebrated Aboriginal Day. The Aboriginal flag of gold, black, and yellow flew, to the consternation of Old Australians, side by side with the national flag on Sydney Town Hall, and a march through town was announced, to be followed by a rally at Alexandria Park. Alas, all this went sadly awry. Nobody seemed to know where the march was to begin, or when somebody pulled the flag down from the Town Hall, not everyone seemed to have mastered the rally chant – *'What do we want? Land rights! What have we got? Bugger all!'* – and the arrangements ran so late that when the time came for speeches everyone had gone home. 'They are a *random* people,' was the convincing explanation I was given, when I asked if this was true to coorie form.

By the time I reached Alexandria Park Aboriginal Day seemed to have fizzled out altogether, and all I found was a small huddle of dark-skinned people around an open bonfire, surrounded by litter on the edge of the green. They greeted me with a wan concern, offering me beer out of an ice-bucket, sidling around me rather, and occasionally winking. A small thin boy with cotton wool stuffed in one ear wandered here and there leading a black puppy on a string. Others kicked a football about in the gathering dusk, and around the fire a handful of older men and women looked sadly into the flames. A strong smell of alcohol hung over us, and the man with the bucket urged me quietly, again and again, to have one for the road, dear. Had the rally been a success? I asked. 'Yeah,' they said, and looked into the fire.

I *did* feel sorry for them. They were like last wasted survivors from some primeval holocaust, those memories of their own civilization were aeons ago expunged. Did they have a Sydney all their own, I wondered, long ago near the beginnings of time? Did their flag fly braver then? When I said good-bye and drove away ('Go on, dear, just one') the lights of the downtown tower blocks were shining in the distance: but in the shadows at the edge of the park the bonfire flames were dancing still, and the frail figures of the indigenes moved unsteadily in the flicker.

One morning I went to Iceland, the skating-rink, to watch the Sydney people skating. They did it, as they do most things, very well. Their tall strong frames looked well on the ice. Once more I was struck by the Scandinavian analogy, so Nordic does an Australian look when you put him in cold circumstances, but eventually my attention was gripped by a figure who, it seemed to me, could be nothing else but Aussie.

He was about five years old, blond, lively, tough and unsmiling. He could not, it seemed, actually skate, but he was adept at running about the rink on his blades, and his one purpose of the morning was to gather up the slush that fell off other people's boots, and throw it at passing skaters. This task he pursued with skilful and unflagging zeal. Hop, hop, he would abruptly appear upon the rink, and picking a likely target, staggering his way across the ice, inexorably he would hunt that victim down until *slosh!* the missile was dispatched – and hobble hobble, quick as a flash he was out of the rink again, gathering more material.

I admired him immensely. He hardly ever fell over, he seldom missed, and he did everything with a dexterous assiduity. When I asked him his name he spelt out GORGE with his finger on the rail of the rink; when I asked him if he was enjoying himself he just nodded grimly; and in my mind's eye I saw him thirty years from now, exploding into a company meeting perhaps, with an irresistible take-over, or relentlessly engineering the resignation of a rival under-secretary. I kept my eye firmly on him as I walked out of Iceland, for instinct told me he was assembling slush for me.

Australia was not built by kindness, nor even by idealism. Convicts, not pilgrims, were its Fathers, and Sydney remains rather steelier than it looks. It is not a very sentimental city, and not much given I fear to unrequitable kindness. There is a certain kind of Sydney face, especially among women, which at first sight looks altogether straight, square and reliable, but which examined more carefully (surreptitiously if possible, over the edge of a newspaper from the next table) reveals a latent meanness or foxiness inherited surely, I tell myself in my romantic way, from the thuggery of the penal colonies.

Here are a few graffiti I have jotted down in Sydney: 'CHINKS HIRED, YOU'RE FIRED'. 'WHITE BUT UGLY'. 'THE POLICE KILLED LYOL TITMARCH'. 'NO SCABS OR ASIANS'. 'TURKISH MURDERERS'. Behind the pleasant façade of this city, harsher things are always happening. Inexplicable political scandals excite the newspapers. Numberless Royal Commissions investigate improprieties. Through this apparently egalitarian society stalks a handful of gigantic capitalists, with tentacles that seem to extend into every cranny of city life, and make you feel that whatever you are doing, whether you are buying an ice-cream or booking an airline ticket, you are making the same rich Australians richer yet. Immigrants say that your older Ocker is a terrible bigot still, and even now they tell me a foreign accent often gets snubs and indignities – and not only a European accent, for the favourite Sydney witticism of the day is the New Zealand Joke ('How d'you set up a New Zealander in a small business?' 'Give him a big one, and wait').

Sydney people strike me as essentially cautious or suspicious in their social attitudes. They lack the gift of spontaneous welcome or generosity. They are too easily embarrassed. Invariably smiling and helpful though this citizenry seems, and quite exceptionally polite, I sometimes think that if I were in real trouble, friendless, destitute and passport-less in the streets, I might feel less abandoned in Manhattan. I considered making the experiment as a matter of fact, and presenting myself on the Circular Quay to beg passers-by for my ferry fare: but I remembered that look in the eye of the ladies at the next table, and lost my nerve.

Even now, two centuries after the event, a streak of bad origins is still apparent in Sydney. Truth will out! It has been smudged in the historical memory – if you can believe the Australians, none of the transported convicts ever did anything worse than poach a squire's salmon, or tumble his daughter in the hay. It has been romanticized, too – in the figure of the larrikin for instance, the Sydney street urchin of ballad and anecdote who used to strut picturesquely about these streets in bell-bottom trousers and pointed shoes, fighting merry gang wars and picking pockets. Today it has been varnished over with layer upon layer of gentility and sophistication, but it is there all the same, and if you want to see it plain, try going to the park on a Sunday afternoon, when the Sydney soap-box orators give vent to their philosophies, and the hecklers to their interruptions. In most countries I love these arenas of free expression – they are rich in picaresque episode and eccentricity, and sometimes even in wisdom. I left Sydney's Speakers' Corner though, with a shudder. The free speech was too grossly free, too crudely spiteful, sexist and foul-mouthed. The arguments were bludgeonly, the humour was coarse, and all around the soap-boxes there strode a horribly purposeful figure, wearing a beret tipped over his eyes, and holding a sheaf of newspaper, whose only purpose was to shout down every speaker in turn, whatever the subject or opinion, with a devastating loutishness of retort – never silent, never still, hurling offensive gibes at speaker and audience alike with a flaming offensive energy.

Now where, said I to myself, have I seen that fellow before? And with a pang I remembered: GORGE the indefatigable ice-slosher, up at the ice-rink.

After lunch one day (Warm Salad, new to me, with Chicken

Liver) I met Kev in the elevator, with three of his friends from the office. They stood there in silence, sometimes shifting on their feet. 'I've just eaten', I ventured for conversation's sake, 'a plate of Warm Salad,' but it did not make them smile. They looked at me anxiously, trying hard to think of a reply. 'Good,' managed Kev himself at last, and with relief, murmuring polite and embarrassed excuses, they left me at the seventeenth floor.

Away to the west of Sydney, over a long innocuous hinterland of suburbs, neither ugly nor beautiful, neither poor nor rich, with Lebanese laundries, and pubs with names like the Gladstone Arms or the Lord Nelson, and ladies in flowered housecoats exercising their dogs at lunch-time, and pizza houses with blown-up pictures of Vesuvius behind their counters, and streets called Myrtle Street and Merryland Road – out there beyond the Western Suburbs you can see the outline of the Blue Mountains. Snow falls up there sometimes, and log fires burn in resort hotels: and beyond them again, beyond Orange and Dubbo, there begins the almost unimaginable emptiness of Australia, extending mile after mile after mile of scrub, waste and desert into the infinite never-never of the aborigines. Nearly all Australia is empty. Emptiness is part of the Australian state of things, and it reaches out of that wilderness deep into the heart of Sydney itself, giving a hauntingly absent sense to the city, and restricting the responses of advertising executives in elevators.

The scrub is always near. The splodges of green everywhere make this metropolis feel, even now, like an interloper in the wasteland, and people commute daily into Sydney from country that is almost virgin bush. Only just outside the metropolitan limits, up on the Hawkesbury River, are communities that still cannot be reached by road, to which the mail goes out each day on a chugging river-boat, nosing its way among the creeks and channels, between woodlands where wallabies leap and koalas ruminate, to be unloaded on rickety wharfs at hamlets of shacks and bungalows, and hobbled away with by aged oystermen – the air-conditioned towers of Sydney itself hardly out of sight beyond the gum-trees!

The sea everywhere, insidiously entering the city in a myriad inlets, seems a vacuous kind of ocean, which seldom brings the tang of a salt breeze into the downtown streets, and often looks to me indeed like fresh water all the time. The history of Sydney, like the history of Australia, is essentially blank, very little of interest ever having happened here, and there is a sort of bloodlessness even to the very success of the place, and a pallor to its style, and a curious suggestion of muffle even at rush-hour, which reminds one repeatedly of that immense desolation beyond the hills.

This sensation preoccupies many Australian artists, and affects me very strangely. Sometimes in Sydney I feel I am not looking directly at the city at all, but seeing it through glass, or perhaps reflected in a mirror. Its edges seem oddly ill-defined when I am in such a mood, its pellucid light is lacking in refraction, without the opacity of dust, breath, history and regret that hangs on the air of most great cities. The wind seems to have been filtered through some pale mesh of the south. Even the seafood, however imaginatively garnished with strawberries or avocado, seems to lack the tang of the deep sea and the tides. Even the Australian language sometimes sounds to me echo-like, as though it is reaching me from far, far away, or out of another time.

Sydney can be exhilarating, but it is a *moderate* exhilaration. It can stir the heart, but not quite to the point of ecstasy. You do not dance along these streets, or thrill to the beat of the place. Its faces, in repose, are neither kind nor cruel, but just expressionless. People seldom seem surprised in Sydney, and for that matter they are seldom very surprising themselves: though it is astonishing that so grand a place should exist down here at all, so handsome, so complete a metropolis on the edge of nowhere, still it never gives the impression, as other young civic prodigies do, that it has burst irresistibly out of the sub-soil into life.

Here are two old Hungarians walking on a Sydney beach. They wear hats, camel coats and signet rings. They came here half a lifetime ago out of the shambles of Europe, and they have lived happily ever after. They escaped the murder of war and the miseries of Communism to prosper in this peaceful haven of the Antipodes. Their wives are taking coffee at the Cosmopolitan – remember the two in furs, silent over their Camparis? Their sons, daughters and grandchildren are probably out in their boats. They are very lucky, and know it. 'We are very lucky,' they say. 'Sydney is a beautiful city. Australia is the Best Country in the World.' They do not say it *con amore*, though, or even *cantabile*. They seem unlikely to kiss the soil they walk on, or raise their hands in gratitude to the Australian dream. 'Let us hope the world stays in peace,' they simply conclude, as if to say, let's hope our luck lasts out – just give us ten more years, O God of the Southern Sun!

Most people like Australia, but in this city of the numbed reflex, the blank eye, few will open their hearts about the place: just as Kev and his colleagues in the elevator, I feel sure, must have bottled up some frightfully witty retorts about the Warm Salad.

Far up the coasts of Sydney, north and south of the Sydney Heads that form the spectacular portal of Australia, comfortable villas of the well-to-do lie encouched in fig-trees, gums and lawns of buffalo grass. They are seldom ostentatious houses. They are not like the garden palaces of Cap d'Antibes, or the monastically enclosed pads of Hollywood. Though it is true that the Sydney *jeunesse dorée* is given to things like flying by seaplane to take lunch in suburban restaurants, or giving birthday parties for favourite Ferraris, still history, temperament and politics have combined to ensure that this is not a city of conspicuous consumption. Its extremely rich are seldom visible, if only because they are in Europe or California; and its glossiest mansions cannot be seen either, because they are country houses set in 25,000 acres of sheep country somewhere over the hills. All this gives the city an air of calm stability: the very idea of economic collapse, still less revolution, seems preposterous, as I look out of my hotel window now to see the white yachts at play in the harbour, yet another laughing horde of schoolchildren storming the terraces of the Opera House, and Kev at his window in his shirt-sleeves, preparing himself psychologically for the long jog home.

Short of another world catastrophe, I think, this place has reached its fulfilment. This is it. It will probably get richer, it will certainly get more Asian, but aesthetically, metaphysically, my bones tell me I am already seeing the definitive Sydney, the more or less absolute Australia. A few more tower blocks here, an extra suburb there, a louder Chinatown, more futuristic ferry-boats perhaps – otherwise, this is how Sydney is always going to be. That bland pallor of personality will survive, that seen-through-a-glass quality, and visitors from the north will always be able to fancy, as they look out at the harbour's odd foliage and wide skies, that they have been deposited upside-down on the obverse of the world. The strain of shyness, the old streak of the brutal, will be held in balance still: another zealot will always be collecting sludge at the ice-rink, another generation of satisfied entrepreneurs will ask destiny for just another decade of happiness, just long enough to live out their lives in the Best Country in the World.

I have been at pains to draw the warts of Sydney in, but on the whole, I have to say, few cities on earth have arrived at so agreeable a fulfilment. Those old Hungarians are right – they are very lucky people, whose fates have washed them up upon this brave and generally decent shore. But just as no man is a hero to his valet, so no city is a paragon to its inhabitants, especially at the end of a hard day in the office, and by 5.30 Kev's morning euphoria has long worn off. The ferries down there are jammed to the gunwales with commuters. The bridge looks solid with traffic. It is drizzling again. Bugger it, Kev remembers, tonight's the night for Andrew and Marge – avocados again, you can bet your life, and they'll probably bring that snotty brat Dominic to crawl around the table. 'Night, Mr Evans.' Night, Avril, silly cow. 'Night, Kev.' Night, Jim, you pot-bellied Ocker. 'Just before you go, Kev, heard this one? There's this New Zealander . . .'

Jeez, this rain is miserable. Get out of the road, you silly sod. Christ, who dreamed up that Opera House? (We all know who paid for it, don't we.) Avocado and prawns, you can bet your life. What was that woman on about in the elevator? Warm Salad! Shit! Look at that traffic! Look at that madman in the Fairmont! Who'd live in a town like this, I ask you. Warm Salad! We must all be bloody loonies . . .

'Kev! Kev, is that you? Marge and Andrew are here, dear, and they've brought little Dominic with them.'

A Baleful Parable

VIENNA, 1983

I first knew Vienna at the very end of the Second World War, but for nearly forty years I never wrote about it. When at last I did, though I gratefully recognized the city's pleasures, I simply could not bring myself to like it. It is no place for a Welsh republican.

Nothing so becomes a city as a street-car (or a tram, as we Europeans prefer it), especially if it has a single cyclopean headlamp on its front, and a couple of flags fluttering on its roof, and is connected by sundry pipes and couplings with a trailer-car behind. What weight! What responsibility! What reassurance!

And nowhere does the tram fulfil its municipal functions more staunchly than in the city of Vienna, for here it must trundle its way, day in day out, come war come peace, through a state of affairs utterly alien to the instincts of any self-respecting trolley: fantasy is piled upon fantasy in Wien, Österreich, pretence is compounded by delusion, introspection repeatedly degenerates into complex, and the whole adds up to a baleful parable of the urban condition. In some ways Vienna is the most intensely civic of great cities, the most complete and compact, the most preoccupied with its own civicness – a fifth of the entire Austrian population, after all, lives within this peculiar capital. In other ways it transcends mere city status altogether, and is more a temperament or a sensibility, embodying as it does an inexpungable repertoire of doubts, regrets and ambiguous prides – was it not within living memory the seat of the Habsburgs, the Imperial

Capital of Austria-Hungary, the root of all that the word 'Empire' came to mean to the world before the wars?

Steadily notwithstanding, small flags flying, the trams clank their way around town: they are painted in strong and sensible colours, and look rather barge-like, as though they ought to be stirring up bow-waves along the track in front of them.

Down upon their diligent passings stare the structures of the Ringstrasse, the boulevard which, in the nineteenth century, replaced the ancient ramparts around the inner city of Vienna. Now as then, the Ringstrasse unforgettably dramatizes the false and footling values of this city, and it has given its name to a whole genre of Viennese art and thought – the Ringstrasse genre. Like some mad architect's dream fulfilled, its buildings rise one after another preposterously into view, Gothic or Grecian or Baroque, plastered in kitsch or writhing with classical allusion, capped by spires, monstrous domes and silhouetted effigies, clumped with goddesses, chariots, gross escutcheons, caryatids, piles of sculpted trophies – here a titanic opera house, here a refulgently Attic Parliament, a university more utterly academic than Princeton, Padua, Cambridge and the Sorbonne put together, museums as overwhelmingly museumy as museums possibly could be, and dominating the whole ensemble, half-way round the ring, the immense pillared sprawl of the Hofburg, the palace of the Habsburgs until their removal after the First World War, which seems to lie there all but exhausted, as well it might, by the weight of so much consequence.

Vienna is all consequence. It stands at the far end of the Alps like a grandiloquent watchman of history. Its streets lead not just to suburbs or provincial towns, but to ancient satrapies and fields of action: the Ostautobahn strikes grandly out for Budapest and Prague, Triesterstrasse will take you, if you persevere, direct to Dalmatia, and at the end of Landstrasse, as Metternich once observed, Asia itself begins. Everything around here is designed for consequence. The Danube passes a mile or two from the Ringstrasse, crossed by strategic bridges, commanded by castles. Flatlands just made for tanks or cavalry sweep away almost from the suburbs to the marshlands of the east. The spire of St Stephen's Cathedral, plumb in the middle of the inner city, stands as a mighty marker to guide or warn the tribes, the caravans and the warring armies.

God-made then for consequence, long ago the city came to worship it. Under the aegis of the immemorially self-important Habsburgs, the Viennese became the archetypal sychophants of history, and made of their city one vast tribute to the vulgarity of class. How could they help it? For centuries they revered as their models of behaviour men who not only called themselves, in all seriousness, Their Imperial, Royal and Apostolic Majesties, but also claimed to be Kings of Jerusalem, Dalmatia, Bohemia, Transylvania, Croatia and Galicia, Grand Dukes of Tuscany, Princely Counts of Tyrol, dukes of a score of dukedoms and lords of lordships without number. These walking Social Registers, these Grand Panjandrums of Central Europe, were the presiding spirits of this place almost into modern times, and their silly standards and superstitions linger inescapably still.

It reminds me of Beijing. Beijing too has torn down its medieval walls to make way for pompous squares and thoroughfares, it too apparently depends for its self-assurance upon childish charades of grandeur, and it is also haunted by the ghosts of dead autocrats. Franz Josef, the last of the great Habsburgs, was the Mao of nineteenth-century Austria, the

Helmsman of Vienna, the Great Father, and like Mao he has left behind him a host of followers who may deny their loyalty to his ideology, but who are subject by hereditary brainwash to his values. Watch now – stand back – here come a couple of Ministers down the steps from the Council Chamber in Parliament, portly important men, deep in portly and important matters of State – and swoosh, like a rocket from his office leaps the porter, buttoning his jacket – out of his door, panting heavily, urgently smoothing his hair, down the steps two at a go, *bitte, bitte!* – just in time, my goodness only just in time to open the door for Their Excellencies, who acknowledge his grovel only with slight inclinations of their heads, so as not to interrupt the flow of the discourse, as they lumber out beneath the figures of Minerva and her attendant sages to their waiting limousine.

Where sundry passers-by look almost inclined to bow and curtsey themselves, to see those dignitaries so lordly! In manners as in symbolisms, Franz Josef's convictions of hierarchy seem to colour everything in Vienna still. Though this is the capital of a republic, and a Second Republic at that, it abounds in princes and archdukes, not to mention mere counts or baronesses, glittering in restaurants with sleek golden hair and predatory half-Magyar faces, elegantly cordial at cocktail parties ('If you're ever in Carinthia, we happen to have a little place down there . . .'), or sometimes to be glimpsed, if young enough, driving around the Ringstrasse in racy Italian cars for all the world as though they should still be dressed in the shakoes, plumes and dangling scabbards of White Hussars.

And below the aristocrats, the social order is marshalled still in self-perpetuating gradations of esteem and respectability. The style of the imperial bureaucracy, established to administer a dominion that extended from Switzerland to Albania, now orders the affairs of a powerless neutral republic of 7½ million souls. People grumble constantly about the size, the slowness, the fussiness, the not unknown corruption, the ornate arcanum of it, but still one feels they are themselves oddly complicit to its survival. It is the last blur of their greatness. It is Franz Josef himself living fuzzily on, honoured still by all Vienna's myriad ranks of social and official import, all its Excellencies and Herr Professors and Frau Doktors and guilds and orders and infinitesimal nuances of protocol – the allegiance symbolized every morning, to this day, by the awe-struck deference that attends the morning exercises of the Imperial Lipizzaner horses, cantering round and round their palatial riding school, and followed obsequiously by a functionary with a shovel to remove their noble defecations.

Vienna feeds upon its past, a fond and sustaining diet, varied with chocolate cake or boiled beef with potatoes (Franz Josef's favourite dish), washed down with the young white wine of the Vienna Woods, digested, and re-digested, and ordered once more, over, and over, and over again … If it reminds me sometimes of Beijing, sometimes it suggests to me the sensations of apartheid in South Africa. The city is obsessed, and obsessive. Every conversation returns to its lost greatness, every reference somehow finds its way to questions of rank, or status, or historical influence. Viennese romantics still love to wallow in the tragic story of Crown Prince Rudolf and his eighteen-year-old mistress Marie Vetsera, 'the little Baroness', who died apparently in a suicide pact in the country house of Mayerling in 1889. The tale precisely fits the popular predilections of this city, being snobbish, nostalgic, maudlin and rather cheap. I went out one Sunday to visit the grave of the little Baroness, who was buried obscurely in a village churchyard by command of Franz Josef, and was just in time to hear a Viennese lady of a certain age explaining the affair to her American guests. 'But in any case,' I heard her say without a trace of irony, 'in any case she was only the daughter of a bourgeois . . .'

I often saw that same lady waiting for a tram, for she is a familiar of Vienna. She often wears a brown tweed suit, and is rather tightly clamped around the middle, and pearled very likely, and she never seems to be encumbranced, as most of us sometimes are, with shopping bags, umbrellas or toasters she has just picked up from the electrician's. If you smile at her she responds with a frosty stare, as though she suspects you might put ketchup on your *Tafelspitz*, but if you speak to her she lights up with a flowery charm. Inextricably linked with the social absurdity of Vienna is its famous *Gemütlichkeit*, its ordered cosiness, which is enough to make a Welsh anarchist's flesh creep: the one goes with the other, and just as it made the people of old Vienna one and all the children of their kind father His Imperial, Royal and Apostolic Majesty, still to this day it seems to fix the attitudes of this city as with a scented glue – sweetly if synthetically scented, like the flavours you sometimes taste upon licking the adhesives of American envelopes.

There is nothing *tangy* to this city, except perhaps the dry white wines. There is no leanness to it. Even the slinkiest of those patricians, one feels, is going to run to fat in the end, and the almost complete absence, in the city centre, of any modern architecture means that a swollen sense of inherited amplitude seems to supervise every attitude. Though Vienna is ornamented everywhere with eagles, the double-headed eagle of the Dual Monarchy, the single-headed eagle of the Austrian Republic, nowhere could be much less aquiline. Vienna an eyrie! It is more like a boudoir birdcage, and when one morning I saw a seagull circling over the pool at Schönbrunn Palace it was like seeing a wild free visitor from some other continent.

Wildness, freeness, recklessness – not in Vienna! I went to a minor police court one day, and noticing one of the accused studying a road map between hearings asked him if he was planning an escape. 'No,' he said, 'I am deciding the best route to visit my aunt at Graz.' The famous Big Wheel of the Prater funfair, that beloved image of the Viennese skyline, moves with such a genteel deliberation that I felt like kicking it, or scrawling scurrilous graffiti on its benches: the Vienna Woods which are said to have inspired so many artists in their passion for the Sublime represent Nature about as elementally thrilling as a rectory rock garden.

But who would want it otherwise, in this city of the coffee-house, the white-tie Wholesalers' Ball and the merry tavern evening with accordion accompaniment? Vienna is an elderly, comfortable, old-fashioned city. If you want excitement, a student of my acquaintance told me, you must either go to Munich or work up a peace demonstration. More immediately to hand than in almost any other city, Vienna possesses all the sensations and appurtenances of metropolitan existence, the stream of the sidewalk traffic, the great green parks with ponds and cafés in them, the opulence of long-established stores, the plushy banks and crowded theatres, the consoling lights of restaurants gleaming on wet pavements, the glimpses of opera audiences spilling out for gossip and champagne in the intermission, the bookshop after bookshop down the boulevards, the hotels rich in lore and private recipes, the memorials to heroes and historical satisfactions, the newspaper kiosks selling *Le Monde* or *Svenska Dagbladet*, the grand steepled hulk of the cathedral above its square,

the buskers in pedestrian precincts, the winking TV tower, the sleepless trams ... Yet as no other city can, Vienna somehow mutates this glorious distillation of human energy and imagination into something irredeemably domestic and conventional.

I walked one day into the Karlskirche, the most spectacular of Vienna's Baroque churches, which has a dome like St Peter's, a couple of triumphal columns dressed up as minarets, and two subsidiary towers roofed in the Chinese manner. Inside I found a wedding in progress. It was magnificent. The great church seemed all ablaze with light and gilding, rococo saints floated everywhere, the bride and groom knelt side by side before the high altar, and flooding through the building came the strains of a Haydn string quartet, marvellously played and amplified to a crisp and vibrant splendour. Yet all that glory was subtly plumpened or buttoned by Vienna, for when I looked at the faces of the congregation I saw no exaltation there, only a familial complacency, satisfaction with the decorum of the arrangements only slightly tinged by the thought that dear Father would have played that *adagio* with a little more finesse.

For yes, if there is one art that has the power to make *Gemütlichkinder* of them all, it is the inescapably Viennese art of music. To Beethoven, Mozart, Haydn, Liszt, Schubert, Brahms, Bruckner, Mahler and any number of Strausses the Viennese feel a cousinly and possessive relationship. 'I hate going to concerts,' I rashly announced to a Viennese companion over dinner one evening, and our rapport was never quite the same again: and ah! how I grew to dread the quivering pause in the garden of the Kursalon – conductor with bow and violin raised above his head, orchestra poised expectant over their strings, audience frozen with their spoons half in, half out of their ice-creams – that preceded, twenty or thirty times a day, the fruity melody and relentless beat of the Viennese waltz!

I made a pilgrimage, all the same, to the grave of Beethoven in the Grove of Honour, at the central cemetery, the *Zentralfriedhof*. Mozart is commemorated there too, if only retrospectively, his body having unfortunately been dumped in an unmarked pauper's grave, and Johann Strauss the Elder is lapped by cherubim nearby, and Hugo Wolf the *Lieder*-writer, than whom no single human being has ever plunged me into profounder despondency, is among the shrubberies round the corner. Beethoven's tomb was easy enough to find because it had so many wreaths upon it, including one laid that morning, with visiting card attached, by Professor Hisako Kocho, President of the Folk Opera Society of Oita Prefecture (telephone Oita 5386). Yet even this grand sanctuary did not make my heart race, or inspire me to heroic yearnings: for with the gilded lyre upon its headstone, its Old German lettering and its generally metronomic or Edition Peters manner, it reminded me horribly of piano practice.

At night however lights are reflected in the overhead wires of the tram-cars, and seem to slide eerily around the Ringstrasse of their own accord, like beings in a separate field of animation, lighter, faster, airier, more sly, than any No. 2 to Franz Josefs-Kai. Perhaps that well-known Viennese Herr Professor Freud used to contemplate them, as he strode on his long meditative walks: certainly it was from the generic psyche of Vienna that he drew his definition of the subconscious – that part of every human, every city, which lies concealed beneath the personality, or is revealed only by shimmering glints on street-car wires.

The most celebrated contemporary citizen of Vienna is not an analyst of trauma, but a scourer. Policeman lounging feet up on the stairs outside, files of data stacked macabre around him,

Simon Wiesenthal the Nazi-hunter sits in his office above Salztorstrasse, close to the old Jewish quarter and the Gestapo HQ, endlessly considering the darkest categories of *Angst*. Around him are framed testimonials from grateful institutions – he is an Award-Winning Nazi-hunter – but few of them come from societies in Vienna. Hundreds of the most virulent Nazis, he says, still live unscathed in these parts – one much-respected builder of churches not only constructed the Auschwitz gas chambers, but *repaired* them, too. Dr Wiesenthal is by no means sufficiently *gemütlich* for the Viennese. There was an attempt on his life not long ago, and the city authorities very much wish, he tells me, that he would go somewhere else: in the meantime they put that slovenly policeman on his door, and another one, toting an automatic rifle, stands just in case outside the Synagogue in Seitenstettengasse.

I have to say that for a few hours after visiting Dr Wiesenthal I saw the face of Eichmann all around me – that peaked but ordinary face which I remember so exactly from the court-room at Jerusalem years ago, and which Hannah Arendt characterized for ever as expressing 'the banality of evil'. Nothing could be more unfair, I know, to the people of Vienna. Half of them are too young to remember Nazidom anyway, and the others, though if we are to believe Dr Wiesenthal they include a far higher proportion of war criminals than survive in any German city, were doubtless the victims above all of their *genii loci*. It was the presence of Vienna, after all, that first incited Adolf Hitler himself to his grandiose dreams of sovereignty – like an enchantment out of the Arabian Nights, he thought the vainglorious horror of the Ringstrasse.

But even if I dismiss from my mind the image of that lady in the brown suit, braided and blonde in those days, greeting the stormtroopers with rose petals from the pockets of her dirndl, still I cannot dispel the feeling, as I walk these streets, that I am promenading one great conglomeration of neurosis.

The reasons for it are not hard to conjecture – the crippling social legacies of the monarchy, the relentless pressures of *Gemütlichkeit*, historical humiliation, geographical exposure – drive down Metternich's Landstrasse now, and in an hour you are on the frontiers of Czechoslovakia or of Hungary, where the sentinels of the Eastern world, weapons over their shoulders, stand with the great steppes at their backs.

No wonder this is a Freudian city in every sense. Not only is Freud's house in Berggasse maintained as a shrine, where you may buy mounted photographs of his original Couch, or fancy yourself summoning dreams for interpretation in the very room where the Oedipus complex was first isolated. Not only that, but everywhere in the city you feel around you the ideas, the idioms and the subject matter of Freud's vision: Father Figures tower in royal and apostolic statuary, libidos search for discos or Prater prostitutes, repressions wander arm-in-arm on Sunday afternoons down the beckoning avenues of *Zentralfriedhof*. It is as though at heart this whole famous metropolis, through its bows, smiles and proprieties, would like nothing so much as to flop down on a sofa in tearful revelation – in the presence, of course, of a properly *gemütlich* and well-qualified Herr Dr Professor.

And the last and most marvellous flowering of the Viennese genius, that surge of styles, ideas and mannerisms which orchestrated the decay and collapse of the Habsburgs, was itself a distinctly neurotic blossoming. No lyric joy of liberation seems to have inspired the new artistic forms by which the architects, the painters and the composers of this city rebelled against the old order of things. The temple of their revolution was the art gallery called the Secession House, built by the architect Josef Olbrich in 1898 and still as good as new: but it was officially opened by the Emperor anyway, and with its squat hunched form and its dome of gilded laurel-leaves looks rather like a mausoleum from that Grove of Honour (though I dare say the Secessionists themselves, whose text was Ver Sacrum, Sacred Spring, thought it looked like a pumproom). There was not, it seems, much fine careless rapture to this renaissance, to the venomous furies and gold-encased women of its paintings, to the alternate swirls and severities of its ever more loveless architecture.

But it did have a daemonic fire to it, and this strain of tormented or inverted genius lingers today like a reflected glow of the city's inner conflicts. I find it more haunting, if less dazzling, than the excesses of Ringstrasse, for it shows itself more obliquely, in art as in life: a sudden tangle of decoration, a blank façade of concrete, the sunken eye of a man in the subway, a woman's twisted face – wrenched by stroke? by bitterness? – as she sits alone over her coffee. For all its comfort, for all its beauty, for all its wealth and self-esteem, Vienna does not feel to me a happy city. Its citizens seem to be still working out, in their various ways, the very same doubts and frustrations which those artists expressed with such disturbing power in the last days of the old regime.

They often fail. The suicide rate has always been high in Vienna. 'He died like a tailor,' is supposed to have been Franz Josef's odious comment on the fate of his son and heir at Mayerling, and so he acknowledged how commonplace, how workaday, was the self-destructive urge among his children the citizens at large. Death is a born Viennese, and nowhere is he more *gemütlich*, as it happens, than in the crypt of the Church of the Capuchins, where the corpses of the Habsburgs themselves 87 are stored: for there is a small workshop down there too, for the restoration of imperial sarcophagi, and if you look through its window you may see a gigantic casket emptied of its contents, having its lid repaired perhaps, or its supporting angels recapitated, and looking for all the world like a car in for its 6,000-mile service, or a lawnmower parked among the buckets and hose-pipes of the garden shed.

I was walking up Kohlmarkt one morning when there appeared beneath the carriage arch of the Hofburg, stalking into the city with a slow imperial swagger, a well-known eccentric of Vienna, nicknamed Waluliso. He was extremely thin, spectral almost. Dressed all in white, as in a toga, he wore an imperial laurel round his brow, and carried a long staff to which streaming banners were attached. As he walked he shouted high-pitched slogans, slip-slopping in his sandals out of the great shaded archway into the sun. Nobody seemed surprised. A policeman chaffed him, a youth on a bicycle slowed down to pat him affectionately on the shoulder: but he gave me a nasty shock, emerging there so abruptly, so white, so skeletonic, so like the ghost of an All-Highest gone off his head with the folly of things, and sprung from his crypt to confuse us.

Actually the trams all but killed me once. In some parts of the Ringstrasse they alone run against the flow of the traffic, and looking to the right to make sure I was not run down by an archduke in an Alfa, I was all but squashed by a trolley-car coming up from the left. '*Achtung! Achtung!*' screamed several ladies in brown tweed suits, but they forgave me my stupidity – had not Dr Waldheim, they reminded each other, Secretary-General of the United Nations, almost met his end in the very same way, on that very same street?

Inevitably people have seen Freud's Death-Wish exemplified in this city, so preoccupied with the past, the tomb, and how the mighty fall. It seems to me though that Vienna is adept at transferring that Wish to others. It is fateful not so much to itself as to the rest of us. It prospers well enough in its neuroses – it is we who suffer the traumas! Viennese Modernism hardly touched the surface of Vienna with its shapes, but everywhere else it was to cause a tragic alienation between architecture and public taste. Viennese Atonalism may seldom be heard in Vienna's own *Musikverein*, but everywhere else it long ago made life's hard pleasures harder still. Viennese Communalism, expressed in the vast housing estates so dear to sociologists of the 1930s, turns out to have been a step towards the universal miseries of the Social Security tower block. The anti-Semitism of Vienna pushed us all towards the Final Solution, the Zionism that was born there has left many a young body, Jewish and Gentile too, dead along the path to Israel. Freud himself, though until twenty years ago, I am told, his name was scarcely mentioned at psychiatry seminars in Vienna, long ago left the rest of the world irrevocably addled by his genius.

Is there any city more seminally disturbing? It is as though Vienna has been a laboratory of all our inhibitions, experimenting down the generations in new ways of confusing us. Perhaps rather than all our Death-Wishes it expresses all our schizophrenias? I rather think it may, you know, for as I stepped back from the track that day just in time to avoid extinction – *Achtung! Stop! Comes the tram!* – I looked up at the passing streetcar and distinctly saw there, just for a moment, my own face in its slightly steamed-up window. We exchanged distant smiles, as between Id and Ego, or dream and wake.

MARTIN AMIS · *God's Dice*
HANS CHRISTIAN ANDERSEN · *The Emperor's New Clothes*
MARCUS AURELIUS · *Meditations*
JAMES BALDWIN · *Sonny's Blues*
AMBROSE BIERCE · *An Occurrence at Owl Creek Bridge*
DIRK BOGARDE · *From Le Pigeonnier*
WILLIAM BOYD · *Killing Lizards*
POPPY Z. BRITE · *His Mouth will Taste of Wormwood*
ITALO CALVINO · *Ten Italian Folktales*
ALBERT CAMUS · *Summer*
TRUMAN CAPOTE · *First and Last*
RAYMOND CHANDLER · *Goldfish*
ANTON CHEKHOV · *The Black Monk*
ROALD DAHL · *Lamb to the Slaughter*
ELIZABETH DAVID · *I'll be with You in the Squeezing of a Lemon*
N. J. DAWOOD (TRANS.) · *The Seven Voyages of Sindbad the Sailor*
ISAK DINESEN · *The Dreaming Child*
SIR ARTHUR CONAN DOYLE · *The Man with the Twisted Lip*
DICK FRANCIS · *Racing Classics*
SIGMUND FREUD · *Five Lectures on Psycho-Analysis*
KAHLIL GIBRAN · *Prophet, Madman, Wanderer*
STEPHEN JAY GOULD · *Adam's Navel*
ALASDAIR GRAY · *Five Letters from an Eastern Empire*
GRAHAM GREENE · *Under the Garden*
JAMES HERRIOT · *Seven Yorkshire Tales*
PATRICIA HIGHSMITH · *Little Tales of Misogyny*
M. R. JAMES AND R. L. STEVENSON · *The Haunted Dolls' House*
RUDYARD KIPLING · *Baa Baa, Black Sheep*
PENELOPE LIVELY · *A Long Night at Abu Simbel*
KATHERINE MANSFIELD · *The Escape*

PENGUIN 60s

READ MORE IN PENGUIN

For complete information about books available from Penguin and how to order them, please write to us at the appropriate address below. Please note that for copyright reasons the selection of books varies from country to country.

IN THE UNITED KINGDOM: Please write to *Dept. JC, Penguin Books Ltd, FREEPOST, West Drayton, Middlesex UB7 0BR.*
If you have any difficulty in obtaining a title, please send your order with the correct money, plus ten per cent for postage and packaging, to *PO Box No. 11, West Drayton, Middlesex UB7 0BR.*

IN THE UNITED STATES: Please write to *Consumer Sales, Penguin USA, P.O. Box 999, Dept. 17109, Bergenfield, New Jersey 07621-0120.* VISA and MasterCard holders call 1-800-253-6476 to order all Penguin titles.

IN CANADA: Please write to *Penguin Books Canada Ltd, 10 Alcorn Avenue, Suite 300, Toronto, Ontario M4V 3B2.*

IN AUSTRALIA: Please write to *Penguin Books Australia Ltd, P.O. Box 257, Ringwood, Victoria 3134.*

IN NEW ZEALAND: Please write to *Penguin Books (NZ) Ltd, Private Bag 102902, North Shore Mail Centre, Auckland 10.*

IN INDIA: Please write to *Penguin Books India Pvt Ltd, 706 Eros Apartments, 56 Nehru Place, New Delhi 110 019.*

IN THE NETHERLANDS: Please write to *Penguin Books Netherlands bv, Postbus 3507, NL-1001 AH Amsterdam.*

IN GERMANY: Please write to *Penguin Books Deutschland GmbH, Metzlerstrasse 26, 60594 Frankfurt am Main.*

IN SPAIN: Please write to *Penguin Books S. A., Bravo Murillo 19, 10 B, 28015 Madrid.*

IN ITALY: Please write to *Penguin Italia s.r.l., Via Felice Casati 20, I-20124 Milano.*

IN FRANCE: Please write to *Penguin France S. A., 17 rue Lejeune, F-31000 Toulouse.*

IN JAPAN: Please write to *Penguin Books Japan, Ishikiribashi Building, 2-5-4, Suido, Bunkyo-ku, Tokyo 112.*

IN GREECE: Please write to *Penguin Hellas Ltd, Dimocritou 3, GR-106 71 Athens.*

IN SOUTH AFRICA: Please write to *Longman Penguin Southern Africa (Pty) Ltd, Private Bag X08, Bertsham 2013.*